MINI
BERLIN

ROUGH GUIDES

How to download your Free eBook

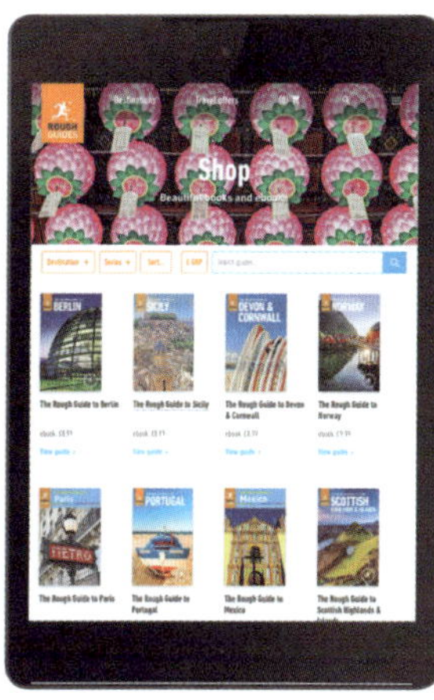

1. Visit **www.roughguides.com/free-ebook** or scan the **QR code** opposite

2. Enter the code **berlin488**

3. Follow the simple step-by-step instructions

For troubleshooting contact: mail@roughguides.com

Contents

Introduction

It's not much of an exaggeration to say that few cities in Europe evoke the continent's modern history more than Berlin. Almost everywhere you look, you will find reminders of the dramatic events of the twentieth century, for Berlin is a city that publicly acknowledges its past, good and bad, through museums, memorials and the preservation of historically significant buildings. At times, this can feel almost overwhelmingly poignant. Yet the vigour with which Berliners embrace the future and their determination to move forward positively while showing respect for the suffering of the past is truly inspiring. A visit to this lively, sophisticated city, which has borne witness to such extremes of human emotion, is an experience that lovers of history and travel alike will not forget in a hurry.

Potsdamer Platz Station

Germany's capital has excited pride for its strength, admiration for its culture, hatred as the centre of Hitler's tyranny, compassion as a bastion of postwar freedom, and fear as a focus of Cold War conflict. More than any other European capital, Berlin symbolises the immense changes wrought through the nineteenth century in Western and Eastern Europe.

For each emotion that the name Berlin evokes, the city

WHEN TO GO

The ideal time to visit Berlin is between Easter and autumn. The city is notorious for its chilly winters, when biting winds from Russia and Scandinavia force its rich cultural life (and its people) indoors for nearly half the year. Visiting during this time makes for a much-diminished visitor experience – there are no boat tours through the networks of waterways that thread through the city centre or on the lakes on its southwest outskirts; some visitor attractions (such as the interiors of the smaller palaces at Potsdam) are closed; and the pleasure of Berlin's parks, gardens and woodlands are denied visitors – whether it's the central wooded Tiergarten, the formal gardens surrounding the palaces at Potsdam and Charlottenburg, or the extensive areas of forest known as the Grunewald that spreads between the lakes and suburbs to the southwest of the city. Sunny days in summer really do enhance the city's appeal for visitors, who can watch the sun set from one of the rooftop lounges in the centre or take the S-Bahn to the end of the line and laze on Europe's busiest inland beach, beside the Wannsee; for these reasons a visit in summer is highly recommended for those who want a thorough experience of the city.

has an appropriate symbol. The noble Schloss Charlottenburg and the monuments on Unter den Linden honour Germany's formidable Prussian past, while the Brandenburg Gate proclaims the city's regained unity. The Reichstag recalls united Germany's return to parliamentary democracy, while the gigantic Olympic Stadium expresses the bombast of Hitler's dictatorship. The chaos and destruction that the Nazis wrought find their deliberate reminder in the bombed-out shell of the Kaiser Wilhelm Memorial Church, while the atrocities of the Holocaust are represented by innumerable memorials big and small. The determination of the Jewish community to forge a stronger identity is best captured by the restored magnificence of the Neue Synagogue.

Relics of the Old Divide

The eastern districts of the city – Mitte, Pankow, Friedrichshain and Prenzlauer Berg – essentially form the old densely populated centre whose tenements (disparagingly referred to as *Mietskasernen*, literally meaning 'rental barracks') inspired the 1920s proletarian theatre of Erwin Piscator and Bertolt Brecht. When Berlin was divided up at the end of World War II, it seemed appropriate that the Soviet sector devoted to the Communist experiment should take in a large number of the working-class areas, while West Berlin had at its centre the eminently bourgeois neighbourhood of Charlottenburg.

With reunification, two sets of people with different psychologies, economies and social systems were suddenly thrust together. Hitherto unforeseen problems emerged. As tens of thousands of East Germans came to settle in the West, entitling them to 'adjustment' money, housing subsidies and job retraining from the Bonn government, the financial burden of reunification now began

OSTALGIE

As the film *Goodbye Lenin!* (2003) illustrates, there are some East Germans for whom reunification proved too much of a shock. Others may have accepted the demise of the German Democratic Republic (GDR), but still look back wistfully on an era that did much good, despite the Communist dictatorship. In their nostalgia for the East (hence the term *Ostalgie*), people hanker for old certainties like jobs for life and workplace kindergartens. Basic items such as food and household products from the GDR are also high on the list. *Ostprodukte* are back in, just like icons that never even left, such as the red-and-green stop/go men, the *Ampelmännchen*, and that most enduring of children's TV characters, the *Sandmännchen*.

A rather different view of the GDR is presented in the book *Stasiland* by Anna Funder and the superb film *The Lives of Others* (2006), both of which examine the impact of state intrusion on personal life.

to trouble West Germans, while a small minority of disgruntled West Berliners even began to wish that the Wall had never come down.

The former site of the Wall, Checkpoint Charlie

Reconstruction and renewal

The collapse of the Wall and the integration of the two independent cities led to a flowering of culture. With no fewer than three opera houses, three major symphony orchestras and two national art galleries, Berlin is justifiably proud of its renewed artistic vigour. The Kulturforum in the Tiergarten was expanded, the magnificent Museumsinsel in the middle of the River Spree was restored, and major new museums such as the Jüdisches Museum opened their doors. Western Berlin's Schaubühne, along with the Berliner Ensemble, Volksbühne and Deutsches Theater from the East, now make up one of the world's most formidable theatrical establishments, promoting both classical tradition and the avant-garde. With the Berlin Film Festival as its flagship, cinema is resuming the excitement of its great creative period in the 1920s, a time commemorated in the exciting Film Museum Berlin (see page 63).

Some cynical Berliners claim that their city was transformed into Europe's largest building site, post-Wall, but the construction boom yielded office, retail and living space to accommodate a growing population that was boosted by the transfer of

SUSTAINABLE TRAVEL

Germany has a long history of both green party politics and sustainable living. Berlin itself is known for its green startups, while May sees the Greentech Festival (https://greentechfestival.com) with speaker meetings and exhibitions of cutting-edge green tech solutions. It's easy for visitors to Berlin to make their visits sustainable too. For a start, the city's public transport system is efficient and comprehensive and can be used to reach everywhere described in this book; there is absolutely no need for visitors to drive in the city (though some may want to hire a bike to get around; see page 126). Although some visitors may have no choice but to arrive by air, there are sustainable options for getting here, with the country's super-fast ICE trains making it entirely feasible to travel to Berlin from London by rail in the space of a day.

When looking for a place to stay or eat, many hotels and restaurants are placing an emphasis on sustainability, with less plastic, more locally sourced produce, less food wastage and more awareness of greenhouse gas emissions; and the vegan and vegetarian restaurant scene is flourishing. For a list of relevant hotels and restaurants, see www.visitberlin.de/en/eco-hotels-sustainable-accomodation-berlin or www.visitberlin.de/en/vegetarian-vegan-cuisine; eco-conscious visitors will also be interested in the RECUP scheme (https://recup.de), where customers pay a small deposit (usually €1 for cups and €5 for bowls) when they buy a drink or food in a RECUP container – the deposit is refunded when the container is returned to any of the many participating locations throughout Berlin.

In terms of shopping, the Nochmall second-hand shopping emporium (www.nochmall.de) in the north of the city is great for a browse for those who want to encourage recycling.

government ministers and civil servants from Bonn to Berlin. Some of the buildings are remarkably beautiful, and the city almost feels like a living art gallery. The Reichstag, once more the seat of unified Germany's parliament, was topped with a huge glass dome, which is supposed to represent the lack of secrecy in modern

German government. Daimler-Chrysler and Sony brought about a quite extraordinary transformation of Potsdamer Platz, and shops, offices and apartments rose from the former Checkpoint Charlie. Gleaming shopping malls full of designer stores were constructed around Friedrichstraße, and old, dilapidated buildings in the east of the city were transformed into art galleries, exclusive fashion boutiques and trendy cafés. A particular hotspot of this kind is Scheunenviertel, north of Hackescher Markt S-Bahn station, where all signs of former economic deprivation have vanished.

Breathing space

Despite its stone, steel and glass, Berlin is the greenest metropolis in Europe, with almost 40 percent of its area occupied by lakes and rivers, parkland and woods. Besides the Tiergarten and the River Spree in the city centre, the southwest suburbs have the forest of the Grunewald, the River Havel and the Wannsee, while the north has the Tegel forest and lake. Small garden colonies abound, with flourishing farming communities, such as Lübars, set inside the city boundaries. To all of this, eastern Berlin adds Großer Müggelsee as well as the woods and parkland around Treptow and Köpenick.

The Memorial to the Murdered Jews of Europe

WHAT'S NEW

Berlin is a city in a constant state of renewal. This is seen nowhere better than in the grandiose building known as the Humboldt Forum (see page 69), the controversial successor to the 1970s Palast der Republik (Palace of the Republic). Where the Palast der Republik celebrated communism in glass, concrete and steel, the Humboldt Forum takes its architectural cues from the Stadtschloss (the Palast der Republik's Baroque predecessor). The Humboldt Forum is home to various exhibition and event spaces and two museums, dedicated to Ethnology and Asian Art, which moved here shortly after the building's opening from elsewhere in Berlin.

In fact, it's the extraordinary richness of Berlin's museums that are providing the other notes of change: during the lifetime of this guide brand-new buildings will open hosting museums showing off the Bauhaus school of design and art (see page 37), and separately, twentieth century art, in the new Berlin Modern (see page 52); while the venerable Pergamon Museum (see page 67), one of the world's great cultural-historical museums, will slowly reopen various exhibition halls as its comprehensive re-building programme (planned to stretch into the 2030s) makes steady progress.

The new buildings come with a combined price tag totalling billions – as do the city's other great renewal projects, which are in its infrastructure, still recovering in some ways from the years of division during the Berlin Wall era: in 2020 a new extension to the U5 U-Bahn line was opened, providing a link between two of the city's great gathering points for tourists, namely Alexanderplatz and the Brandenburg Gate, with new stops including one at Museumsinsel, next to the Humboldt Forum; while in the same year the city's brand new airport, Berlin Brandenburg Airport Willy Brandt (see page 125), opened to the southeast of the city, giving visitors who arrive by air the same slick experience as those who come by train, who arrive at the still very futuristic-looking Hauptbahnhof, opened in 2006 but almost two decades later not looking its age at all.

Young at heart

Beyond sightseeing, the most fascinating thing about Berlin is its people. Throughout the city's turbulent history, the individualism, courage and wit of Berliners have elicited the admiration of the watching world. A preconceived notion of Germans as a whole, but Prussians in particular, has often presented them as a cool and unfeeling people. However, such notions are quickly dispelled by the warmth and good humour exhibited by many of the city's people.

Younger Berlin's so-called 'alternative scene' has revived the city's 1920s reputation of lively and wildly independent-minded folk, with the city's relatively low rents drawing creative types galore, although gentrification in recent years is changing even the more radical areas. Also to be found in traditional workingt-class districts like Kreuzberg and Neukölln is Berlin's large community of immigrants, originally called *Gastarbeiter* (guest workers), most of them from Turkey, who add considerable colour and flavour to the city's social and gastronomic life.

This sprawling, invigorating and lively metropolis attracts over 13 million visitors a year, none of whom can help but feel a mixture of privilege and awe at witnessing such an exciting and evolving city.

Café culture in Prenzlauer Berg

10 Things not to miss

1 **CENTER AM POTSDAMER PLATZ**
An entertainment complex at the heart of Potsdamer Platz. See page 53.

2 **GENDARMENMARKT**
A grand square dominated by twin cathedrals. See page 63.

3 **SCHLOSSBRÜCKE**
With its fine sculptures, this is Berlin's most beautiful bridge. See page 65.

4 **THE REICHSTAG**
See Berlin from the iconic parliament building. See page 45.

5 **BRANDENBURG GATE**
The enduring symbol of Berlin. See page 57.

6 **SANSSOUCI**
Stroll around the palace gardens. See page 88.

7 **SCHLOSS CHARLOTTENBURG**
A Baroque and Rococo masterpiece. See page 76.

8 **THE PERGAMONMUSEUM**
See awe-inspiring wonders of the ancient world. See page 67.

9 **OLYMPIASTADION**
Imposing and magnificent venue built for the 1936 Olympic Games. See page 80.

10 **JEWISH MUSEUM**
Tragic history and moving stories. See page 63.

A Perfect Day in Berlin

9AM

Breakfast. A reservation at Käfer (see page 120), the rooftop restaurant in the Reichstag, is a civilised way to avoid the long queues to go up to the glass dome.

10AM

Morning walk. Stroll through the symbolic Brandenburg Gate and down Unter den Linden. Take a detour to the Holocaust Memorial to absorb the undulating pillar landscape and its significance.

12 NOON

Retail therapy. Turn into Friedrichstraße for a spot of shopping on Berlin's designer mile. Take a look at the huge multicoloured sculpture in the Quartier 205 Stadtmitte shopping centre and stop for lunch in its excellent food court.

2PM

River cruise. Head up to the Schiffbauerdamm boat landing at Weidendammer Brücke for a cruise along the River Spree. The shortest tours last around an hour and take in the government quarter, plus other Berlin highlights.

4PM

Café culture. Walk back to Unter den Linden to sample some delightful cakes at the popular Café Einstein, then stroll east and choose one of the museums on Museumsinsel to look around.

5PM

Futuristic buildings. Explore the modern architecture in the Center am Potsdamer Platz (formerly the Sony Center; the U-Bahn will get you there, via a change at Brandenburger Tor) and take in more retail therapy at the Playce, across the road, the three-storey glass-roofed shopping centre designed by star architect Renzo Piano.

5PM

Sunset panorama. Shuttle up Kollhoff Tower at Potsdamer Platz on Europe's fastest lift for a perfect sunset view from the two-floor observation deck. Similar views are provided from the late-opening Solar Sky-Bar and Restaurant (Stresemannstraße 76; cross the back yard to find the glass lift).

7PM

Time for dinner. Dine at one of the many restaurants around Potsdamer Platz – perhaps in the Center am Potsdamer Platz, where you can eat while marvelling at the spectacular architecture.

9PM

On the town. Explore Berlin's nightlife. A good place to start is the KulturBrauerei, a converted old brewery in Prenzlauer Berg with limitless other club and bar options within walking distance (the U2 underground line takes you there; get off at Eberswalder Straße and walk down Schönhauser Allee to Sredzkistraße).

On the Trail of the Berlin Wall

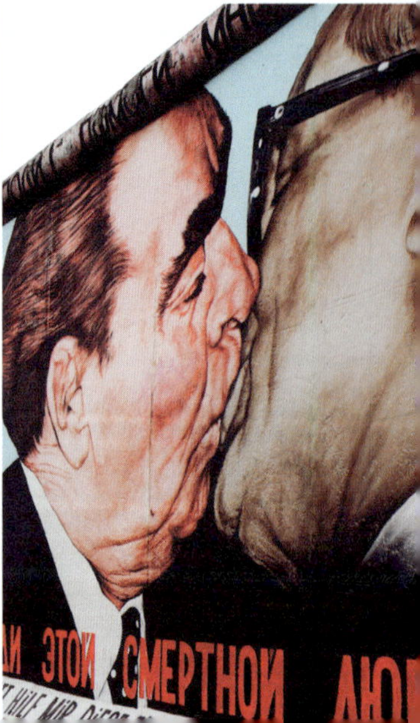

9AM

Breakfast. Start the day at Café Libre (around 200m west of Bernauer Strasse U-Bahn). The café is situated on the site of the former Wall and will set you up for a day's look at the reminders of the notorious division of Berlin between 1963 and 1989.

10AM

Berlin Wall Memorial. The Memorial (Gedenkstätte Berliner Mauer), stretches for over a kilometre along Bernauer Strasse from Café Libre to Nordbahnhof S-Bahn. Take in the remaining sections of the wall, the memorials to those who died attempting to cross it, and the strikingly modern Chapel of Reconciliation (Kapelle der Versöhnung).

11AM

Bernauer Strasse Interpretation Centres. The Dokumentationszentrum Berliner Mauer provides a comprehensive account of the Wall's history, with a lookout point over the site. Before heading off on the S-Bahn, take a look at the exhibition in the station that documents how escapees tried to use the S-Bahn tunnels in their bid for freedom.

1PM

Checkpoint Charlie. Travel by S-Bahn and U-Bahn to the site of Checkpoint Charlie, one of the former border crossing points on the wall. The US army hut and the sign notifying you that you are 'Leaving the American Sector' provide classic photo-ops; after that, there's a museum dedicated to the checkpoint, a further museum about the Cold War, and an unusual diorama showing life on both sides of the wall in the 1980s. 200m further on along Zimmerstrasse a remaining stretch of the wall can be seen outside the Topographie des Terrors (one of the city's museums dedicated to the Nazi era). Head to the nearby Japanese restaurant, Ishin (www.ishin.de/en) for a reasonably-priced late lunch.

4PM

East Side Gallery. A trip by U-Bahn to Warschauer Strasse allows for a look along a remaining stretch of the Berlin Wall that runs alongside the River Spree, which graffiti artists have made their own; wall art in the 'East Side Gallery' includes the famous picture of Soviet premier Leonid Brezhnev embracing his East German counterpart Erich Honecker.

6PM

Evening meal. To see a very different legacy of the old East Germany, head for the Nikolaiviertel, southwest of Alexanderplatz; there's no sign of the wall here but plenty of places to eat along the riverside including Zille-Stube (see page 121) and the Brauhaus Georgbraeu (see page 119). This area was rebuilt by the East German government to give an impression of how Berlin looked in medieval times, in advance of the 750th anniversary (in 1987) of the city's founding.

Berlin's Great Outdoors

9AM

Breakfast in the Tiergarten. Start the day's jaunt through Berlin's abundant wide open spaces at the Café am Neuen See in the southwestern part of the Tiergarten, the famous area of woodland, parkland and lakes in the heart of the city. The café is right beside its namesake lake and is a gorgeous, secluded spot to enjoy coffee and breakfast. Then it's time to head around the Tiergarten itself – maybe stopping off at the Rose Garden (Rosengarten), the English Garden to the north, and the Siegessäule Victory Column, which lies at the heart of the park (a climb to the top allows for a superlative view across the Tiergarten and beyond).

11AM

On foot through the Grunewald Forest. Take the S-Bahn out to Wannsee and with the aid of a good map follow the network of paths that lead from the S-Bhan station past the Strandbad Wannsee (beach) and then along the shore of the Wannsee and then a quieter lake, the Havel, until you reach the Grunewaldturm (see page 84), a striking brick-built lookout tower set back a little from the lake shore, amidst the trees (total length: around 10km/6.2 miles). The Wannseeterrasen (www.wannseeterrassen.berlin) by the beach or Kaiser Garten am Grunewaldturm (https://info996594.wixsite.com/website) at the foot of the lookout tower can provide an early or late lunch of German specialities, as desired. From the lookout tower, you can catch the bus back to Wannsee S-Bahn station.

4PM

A walk through Park Sanssouci. Park Sanssouci in Potsdam is the area of formal parks and gardens established by Frederick the Great around his great Baroque palaces; wooded glades merge into woodland and more formal areas of landscaped gardens, and the whole place is free to walk in. From Potsdam station there's a bus to the Neues Palais (see page 89) where you can pick up a map of the park at the visitors centre and make your way through it however you wish – there's plenty to discover by way of small schlosses fronted by fountains and the not-so-small Orangerie; the finishing place to aim for is the Friedenskirche bus stop for a bus back to Potsdam town centre. The overall distance will depend on the route you take, but reckon on around 2–3km (1.2–1.9 miles).

6PM

Evening meal in Potsdam. The elegant town of Potsdam is adjacent to the Park, and any restaurant in the centre, marked by Gutenbergstrasse and its intersections with Lindenstrasse and Dortustrasse, will find favour with hungry walkers after their day spent exploring Berlin's surprisingly extensive outdoors.

History

Today's Berlin originated from the settlements of Cölln (founded in 1237; the name survives in the modern borough of Neukölln) and Berlin (founded in 1244). The two formed a unity in the early 1300s, and by 1432 had formally merged into the twin town of Cölln-Berlin.

Berlin continued as a virtually autonomous outpost until the accession of Brandenburg's Kurfürst (Prince Elector) Friedrich II in 1440. Quarrels broke out between the city's citizens and Friedrich II, culminating in the so-called *Berliner Unwillen* in 1448, which resulted in Berlin losing many of its rights and privileges.

Prussia and Napoleon

With his ambition of uniting the states of Brandenburg and Prussia, it was the Great Elector Friedrich Wilhelm (1640–88) who fortified Berlin as a garrison town. The first newcomers were fifty wealthy Jewish families who had been expelled from Vienna in 1671. Then, 14 years later, 5,600 Huguenot Protestants arrived after being driven out of France by the revocation of the Edict of Nantes. At a time when France was considered the cultural master of Europe, these sophisticated merchants and highly skilled craftsmen – among them jewellers, tailors, chefs and restaurant owners – brought a new refinement to the town.

This refinement was further enhanced by the Great Elector's son, also called Friedrich, who, during his long reign as Elector of Brandenburg (1688–1713), crowned himself King Friedrich in (not *of*) Prussia. Prompted by Sophie Charlotte, his wife, the king founded academies for the arts and sciences in Berlin. Baroque master

NOTES

Living was easy in fifteenth-century Berlin, as historian Johannes Trithemius noted: 'Life here consists of nothing but eating and drinking'.

Andreas Schlüter (see page 67) was commissioned to redesign the royal palace (Stadtschloss). Badly damaged in World War II, the place was knocked down in 1950, making way for East Germany's Palast der Republik (itself demolished in the Noughties to make way for the Humboldt Forum; see page 69). Sophie Charlotte's residence, however, the grand Schloss Charlottenburg, has been restored as a model of the era's elegance.

Schloss Charlottenburg

Friedrich Wilhelm I (1713–40), the son of Friedrich and Sophie Charlotte, despised the Baroque glitter of his parents' court, and subjected the previously easy-going Berliners to a frugal, rigid concept of *Preussentum* (Prussianness; an unquestioning obedience to the ruler and his administrators) and sharply defined class distinctions, affirming the supremacy of the aristocracy, officer class and soldiers over civilians in general. The Soldier King spent his life in uniform, and his courtiers followed suit. Irascible and deeply religious, he was simple in his tastes, finding the greatest pleasure in strictly male company over a pipe and a tankard of beer; wine struck him as too expensive.

His son Friedrich der Große (Frederick the Great, 1740–86), King *of* (not just *in*) Prussia, took his realm to the forefront of European politics and had little time for Berlin. He concentrated on turning his beloved Potsdam into a mini-Versailles, where French was spoken and Voltaire became his official philosopher-in-residence; his palaces remain a popular excursion from the city to this day (see page 87). He rarely appeared in Berlin except to garner public support – and taxes – after his return from costly wars with the Silesians, Russians and Austrians.

Capital of Germany

After the defeat of Napoleon, the accelerating industrial revolution produced a new Berlin proletariat of 50,000 workers. Demonstrations were held to protest against working and living conditions, but in 1848, they were crushed by the Prussian cavalry, leaving 230 dead. The king made small concessions, paying lip service to the demand for press freedom. A year later, police controls had been tightened, press censorship resumed, and democratic meetings swarmed with government spies.

Prussia's success during the Franco-Prussian War (1870–1871) placed it at the head of a new united Germany. Under Kaiser Wilhelm I and Chancellor Bismarck, Berlin became the *Reichshauptstadt* (capital of the empire). By 1880, amid the industrial expansion of the *Gründerzeit* (founding years), the city's population soared past the million mark. Berlin boomed as the centre of Germany's engineering industry.

After its period of rapid growth, the city began to assume its place as Germany's cultural, as

NOTES

When Friedrich Wilhelm I came to the throne, a wag's graffiti on the palace wall pinpointed the costs of his parents' extravagance: 'This castle is for rent and the royal residence of Berlin for sale'. To pay off the debts, he cut court officials' salaries from 250,000 silver thalers to 50,000, sold the opulent coronation robes, melted down the palace silver, and tore the flowers out of Schloss Charlottenburg Park and replaced them with a far more practical crop: cabbages.

political capital, with Berlin artist Max Liebermann and others challenging Munich's dominance of German painting. The Berlin Philharmonic gained international standing, attracting Tchaikovsky, Strauss and Grieg as guest composers, and in 1905, the Viennese director Max Reinhardt arrived to head the Deutsches Theater.

St. Nicholas Church in the historic quarter of Nikolaiviertel

Among its scientists, Robert Koch won a Nobel Prize for his discovery of the *Tuberculosis bacillus*, and Max Planck headed the new Kaiser Wilhelm Society for the Advancement of Science (later named the Max-Planck-Gesellschaft), with none other than Albert Einstein as director of the physics department.

War and revolution

Berliners originally supported the Kaiser in what proved to be the Hohenzollerns' last military gasp – World War I. But the enthusiasm was short-lived. Privations at home and the horrendous loss of life on the front turned popular feeling against the war. In 1916, Karl Liebknecht and Rosa Luxemburg formed the Spartacus League. Two years later, with Germany defeated, revolution broke out in Berlin. While the Social Democrats were proclaiming a new German republic, Liebknecht took over the palace, declaring the Republic socialist. But Chancellor Friedrich Ebert and his Social Democrats outmanoeuvred

Frederick the Great

the Spartacists, and some 4,000 *Freikorps* (right-wing stormtroopers) were called in to smash the movement; Liebknecht and Luxemburg were both assassinated. Four days later, a new National Assembly was elected, and the dominant Social Democrats moved the government to the safety of Weimar to draw up the constitution of the new republic.

The use of the *Freikorps* to suppress the Spartacists was to haunt the Weimar Republic. In March 1920, the Kapp Putsch brought 5,000 stormtroopers into Berlin with an obscure civil servant, Wolfgang Kapp, installed as puppet chancellor. The coup lasted only five days, but it set the tone for Germany's fragile experiment in parliamentary democracy. The swastika displayed on the helmets of the *Freikorps* was to reappear on the armbands of Hitler's stormtroopers, crushing all democracy in 1933.

The Golden Twenties

The turbulent twenties gave Berlin a special place in the world's popular imagination. In 1920, the incorporation of eight townships and some sixty suburban communities into the metropolis effectively doubled Berlin's population overnight to 4 million. Before democracy was extinguished in 1933, the city led a charmed life of exciting creativity that left its mark on the whole of European culture. Defeat in World War I had shattered the rigid certainties of

Berlin's 'Prussianness' and left the town open to radical adventures in social and artistic expression almost unimaginable in the older cultural capitals of Vienna, London and Paris. One movement that flourished was Dadaism, which was characterised by a rejection of traditional art values and societal norms and the embrace of absurdity, irrationality and nonsense; it found its expression in performance and visual art, sculpture, literature, sound media and radical left-wing politics. In the meantime, nightclubs on Tauentzienstraße provided a combination of political satire and striptease, accompanied by copious amounts of alcohol, cocaine and sexual licence. The paintings of Otto Dix, Georg Grosz and Max Beckmann were brutally realist, and the dissonance of the times was aptly captured by the atonal music composed by Arnold Schönberg and his pupil Alban Berg.

The conservative establishment winced when the Prussian Writers' Academy chose as its president Heinrich Mann (the elder brother of Thomas Mann), a violent critic of the bourgeoisie and a Communist Party supporter. His best-known novel, *Professor Unrat*, inspired Josef von Sternberg's *The Blue Angel* (1930), the film that revealed the vocal talents of Marlene Dietrich.

NOTES

Berlin showed its sense of the times with its mastery of film, the twentieth-century art form. Fritz Lang, F.W. Murnau, G.W. Pabst and Ernst Lubitsch were the leading directors of their generation. While Hollywood had considered cinema to be principally an industry of mass entertainment, the Berlin filmmakers added a new perception of its artistic possibilities with *Lulu* (1917), *The Cabinet of Dr Caligari* (1920), *Nosferatu* (1922) and *M* (1931). After seeing Fritz Lang's premonitory fable of human regimentation, *Metropolis* (1927), Hitler wanted the master of the dark spectacle to make publicity films for him. Lang chose instead to leave for the US.

The Third Reich

Hitler became the chancellor on 30 January 1933. Only a month later, on 27 February, the Reichstag went up in flames. Hitler used the fire as a pretext to eliminate communist and other left-wing opposition from German political life. The Nazi reign of terror had begun.

Flames were the leitmotif of the Third Reich in Berlin. On 10 May 1933, a procession brought thousands of students along Unter den Linden to the square before Humboldt University. They carried books, not to a lecture but to a bonfire on which were burned the works of Thomas Mann, Heinrich Mann, Stefan Zweig, Albert Einstein and Sigmund Freud, as well as Proust, Zola, Gide, H.G. Wells and Jack London. In 1936, a flame was brought from Athens to Berlin to inaugurate the Olympic Games, an attempt at Aryan propaganda which was soundly subverted by Black athlete Jesse Owens, who won four gold medals. In deference to foreign visitors, anti-Semitic signs like *Juden unerwünscht* (Jews not wanted) were removed from shops, hotels and cafés. As soon as the foreigners had left town, the signs went up again.

Discrimination against Jewish people moved inexorably to what would become known as Kristallnacht (the Night of Broken Glass). On the 9–10 November 1938 the Nazis coordinated a wave of nationwide antisemitic violence. The Decree on the Elimination of the Jews from Economic Life was issued only days later.

Berlin's Jewish population, which stood at 170,000 in 1933, was reduced by emigration and extermination to around 6,000 by 1945.

NOTES

A memorial tablet by the Lichtenstein Bridge marks the spot where Rosa Luxemburg's body was thrown into the Landwehr Canal.

World War II

The first bombing raids on Berlin came in 1940 from the British in retaliation for the air raids on London. Attacks were stepped up after the German defeat at Stalingrad in 1943, with Anglo-American carpet-bombing. The worst single raid was on 6 February 1945, when bombs wiped out 4 sq km (1.5 sq miles) of the city centre in an hour. Hitler spent the last days of the war in his bunker at the Reich Chancellery (nothing survives of the bunker today, there's just a parking lot where it once stood, though an information board on Gertrud-Kolmar-Straße tells its story). As Soviet troops moved in to capture the city, he committed suicide with a shot through the mouth.

The Reichstag on fire, February 27, 1933

The war finally ended with the unconditional German surrender on 8 May 1945. In devastated and starving Berlin, the population was left to pick up the pieces – literally. Women formed groups of *Trümmerfrauen* (rubble women), with 60,000 of them taking on the gruelling work of passing the debris of war by hand to clear the ground for rebuilding.

Division and reunification

It was the Soviets who first occupied Berlin. American, French and British troops and administrators did not arrive in the city until some weeks after the German capitulation. Control of Berlin by the four powers was agreed at Potsdam by Winston Churchill, Harry Truman and Joseph Stalin. The Soviet eastern sector covered just under half the city's area; the French, British and Americans divided the western sector between themselves.

The Allies soon found themselves confronted with Soviet efforts to incorporate the whole of Berlin into a communist-controlled eastern Germany. For their part, the Soviets and their East German allies were unhappy that West Berlin's capitalist presence in the middle of East Germany was having a subversive influence on the communist experiment, and they began to restrict traffic from West Germany. In June 1948, all road, rail and waterway routes to West Berlin were sealed off. The Western Allies countered the blockade by airlifting between 4,000 and 8,000 tons of food and other vital supplies into Berlin every day for 11 months. The blockade ended in May 1949, and West Berlin became a *Land* linked administratively with the new Federal Republic of Germany, which had Bonn as its capital. East Berlin was made the capital of the fledgling German Democratic Republic.

Discontent with living conditions in East Berlin first erupted into open revolt on 17 June 1953. Striking workers marched down Stalinallee (soon after renamed Karl-Marx-Allee) to demonstrate against the government of Walter Ulbricht. They were protesting against the state demands for increased productivity, while their standard of living continued to compare poorly with that of West Berlin. Soviet tanks crushed the revolt.

By the end of the 1950s, over 3 million citizens had fled East Germany in search of a better life, over half of them through Berlin. The authorities decided to put a

NOTES

Civilian escapes by tunnel, cars with hidden compartments, and other subterfuges, including by hot-air balloon, became as much a part of the Cold War legend as breakouts by prisoners of war in World War II; the Checkpoint Charlie Museum (see page 62) includes an engrossing account of these escapes.

stop to the haemorrhage. In the early hours of 13 August 1961, the East German military began to erect a barrier that would separate East and West Berlin and change the lives of several million people for almost three decades. The barrier grew from an improvised barbed-wire fence into a concrete wall close to 4m (13ft) high, topped by concrete tubing. Behind it, protected by an electrified fence, stretched a strip of sand 150m (160yd) wide – a no-man's land equipped with watch-towers, patrol dogs and searchlights. The most poignant stretch of the Berlin Wall was in the district of Wedding, where Bernauer Straße ran one side in the east, the other in the west.

Berlin Crisis of 1961, Checkpoint Charlie

For the Western Alliance, the Wall made West Berlin an even more powerful symbol of freedom. On his visit in 1963, US President John F. Kennedy dramatically underlined the Western Allies' commitment to the city with his famous proclamation: '*Ich bin ein Berliner*'.

The final push that led to the collapse of the Berlin Wall came in 1989 when a campaign in Leipzig against nuclear weapons and industrial pollution grew into nationwide pressure for democratic freedom. With thousands of East Germans fleeing to the West via Hungary, Czechoslovakia and Poland, the country was swept up in Eastern European revolutions fuelled by the reforms of Soviet leader Mikhail Gorbachev. His visit to East Berlin in October 1989

Attendees give Hitler the Nazi salute at the Kroll Opera House

for the fortieth anniversary of the GDR left it clear that Soviet troops would no longer prop up its regime. The Berlin Wall was opened on 9 November 1989, and at midnight on 3 October 1990, a huge black, red and gold national flag was hoisted at the Reichstag. East and West Berlin were united once more.

The city today

On 20 June 1991, Berlin's role at the hub of German life was assured when the Bundestag voted by a slim majority to restore it as the seat of government. In May 1999, a federal president was elected at the Reichstag and, in August that year, government business was finally moved back from Bonn to Berlin.

Berlin continued its transformation early in the twenty-first century. The new government quarter was completed, new foreign embassies were opened, and old ones refurbished. Restoration of historic buildings proceeded apace, and the realisation of major schemes such as at Potsdamer Platz made Berlin a showcase for modern design. Striking additions to the city's architectural attractions include the Hauptbahnhof (Central Station); the new Brandenburg airport; and the Humboldt Forum (see page 69).

Despite its reputation for openness and tolerance, Berlin has not been immune to Europe's twenty-first-century troubles. On

December 19 2016, a terrorist acting on behalf of the so-called Islamic State hijacked a lorry and drove it into a crowded Christmas market at Breitscheidplatz, killing twelve people. Thirty years on from the fall of the Wall, with tensions between Germany's welcoming of Syrian War refugees and the renewed rise of right-wing populism, challenges remain for this dynamic capital city.

Chronology

1237–44 First record of Cölln and Berlin.

1300s Cölln and Berlin form a unity.

1440 Friedrich II becomes Prince-elector of the Margraviate of Brandenburg.

1701 Berlin becomes the capital of the kingdom of Prussia.

1740–86 Frederick the Great ascends the throne.

1871 Berlin becomes the capital of the German Empire.

1918 Philipp Scheidemann proclaims a German republic.

1933 Hitler imposes a dictatorship after the Reichstag fire.

1938 Anti-Jewish violence sweeps Germany during the late evening and early morning of 9–10 November.

1940 The RAF bomb Berlin in retaliation for the German bombing of London.

1945 The Four Powers (France, the Soviet Union, the US and Great Britain) divide Berlin into four sectors.

1961 The SED seals the borders around West Berlin with barbed wire and walls.

1989 The Berlin Wall falls.

1990 Reunified Berlin elects first parliament in over forty years.

1991 Berlin again becomes the seat of government.

2020 Berlin Brandenburg Airport Willy Brandt opens.

2021 Olaf Scholz replaces Angela Merkel as chancellor

2024 The Olympiastadion in Berlin hosts the The UEFA Euro 2024 final.

2025 Berlin hosts the 75th Berlin International Film Festival

Museumsinsel (Museum Island)

Places

You'll need to plan carefully for a thorough exploration of Berlin; covering 880 sq km (340 sq miles), it is larger in area than most European capitals. However, it only just scrapes into lists of top ten cities on the continent by population – the expansive amount of greenery is a real feature of the city, and also the controlling factor in its comparatively low population density. Virtually the whole of the city is accessible via public transport, including outlying areas such as Grunewald and Potsdam, and there is absolutely no need for a car in Berlin.

A good orientation exercise is to start with an organised sightseeing tour, either by bus or, even more leisurely, by boat along the River Spree, River Havel and neighbouring lakes and canals; see pages 44 and 84 for more details.

This guide takes in the sights of Central Berlin from west to east, starting at the Kurfürstendamm, then on to the Tiergarten area, and through the Brandenburg Gate to Unter den Linden and eventually Alexanderplatz, once the heart of the historic city.

Around the Kurfürstendamm

Highlights

- **Kranzler Eck**, see page 36
- **Breitscheidplatz**, see page 38
- **The Zoo**, see page 40
- **Tauentzienstraße**, see page 40
- **Wittenbergplatz**, see page 41

West Berlin's main thoroughfare, literally 'Prince Elector's Embankment', is known to Berliners as the **Ku'damm** ❶. It extends for 3.5km (about 2 miles) through the western part of the city centre, and it's here that you will find a vast array of shops, cafés, restaurants,

NOTES

At Fasanenstraße 23, 300m Southwest of Kranzler Eck (and close to Uhlandstrasse U-Bahn) is the Literaturhaus (www.literaturhaus-berlin.de/), where readings, seminars and discussions are held. The villa is surrounded by a delightful garden, and there is a pleasant café, the Café Wintergarten.

theatres, cinemas and art galleries, as well as no-frills fast-food stands and the inevitable souvenir sellers.

Impressed by the prolongation of the Champs-Elysées in Paris to the Bois de Boulogne, Bismarck wanted to extend the Ku'damm out to the Grunewald forest. However, these plans were never realised, and finally, the avenue linked Kaiser Wilhelm Memorial Church to nothing grander than the Halensee railway station.

The avenue lost almost all the Jugendstil architecture of its Wilhelminian heyday during World War II, and only a few vestiges survive. Otherwise, the street is resolutely modern – gleaming glass, steel and an occasional touch of marble – but still a magnet for fashion-conscious shoppers.

Kranzler Eck

Like so much of the city, this neighbourhood is in a constant state of redevelopment. The **Kranzler Eck** (Kranzler Corner), where the city's most stylish citizens once stopped off for coffee and cakes, has been transformed by the addition of a stunning 16-storey glass skyscraper, designed by Helmut Jahn of Chicago and completed in 2002.

Off the Ku'damm at Fasanenstraße 79, you will find the **Jüdisches Gemeindezentrum** (Jewish Community Centre; www.jg-berlin.org/index.html). Framing the entrance is the domed portal from the synagogue, which was burned during Kristallnacht or 'Night of Broken Glass' in 1938 (see page 28). The modern building serves as a cultural centre for the 12,000 Jewish people living in Berlin today – in 1933, they numbered some 170,000.

It is worth exploring some of the other side streets off the Ku'damm. As well as Fasanenstraße, you will discover many other elegant tree-lined boulevards studded with beautiful, balconied villas, antiques shops, art galleries and exclusive designer boutiques. A little to the north, **Savignyplatz** provides a focus for first-class art and architecture bookshops and art galleries, located in the arches beneath the overhead S-Bahn railway line. Here you will find an abundance of literary cafés, bistros and bars, with plenty of outside seating.

Some 800m Northwest of Kranzler Eck, along Hardenbergstrasse and beside Ernst-Reuter-Platz U-Bhan, is the **Museum für Gestaltung/Bauhaus Archiv 2** (Knesebeckstrasse 1; www.bauhaus.

Kranzler Eck shopping mall

de/de/; free), a showcase of architectural and industrial design that focuses on the Bauhaus movement; it will move to a new site on Klingelhöferstraße during the lifetime of this guide (see page 47).

Breitscheidplatz

To the east of the Kranzler Eck, the Ku'damm leads through to **Breitscheidplatz**, a large pedestrianised area at the base of the Europa-Center and a busy gathering place for shoppers and sightseers during the day. In the centre of the square is Joachim Schmettau's granite **Weltkugelbrunnen** (or Fountain of the World), which locals have cheerily christened the Wasserklops ('aquatic meatball').

Christ the King mosaic in the Kaiser-Wilhelm Memorial Church

Soaring above it immediately to the west is an enduringly powerful symbol of the city, the **Kaiser-Wilhelm-Gedächtniskirche** ❸ (Kaiser Wilhelm Memorial Church; www.gedaechtniskirche-berlin.d/; free). The 1943 bombing, combined with artillery fire at the end of the war, left the tower with the broken stump of its spire – 63m (206ft), compared with its original 113m (370ft) – as a monumental ruin recalling the city's destruction. Flanking it on either side, a strikingly modern hexagonal tower and octagonal church built in the 1960s represent the

WHERE TO SHOOT THE BEST PICTURES

Berlin is not a conventionally handsome or photogenic city. Much of the rebuilding that took place after the war (particularly in the former East Berlin) was functional and lacks aesthetic appeal. (An exception is the tight knot of streets around the Nikolaikirche which were rebuilt in the 1980s to emulate the medieval heart of Berlin.) The city even lacks a photogenic river frontage (the banks of the Spree consist largely of rather ponderous nineteenth-century buildings). A final issue to look out for is the weather. Unfortunately, Berlin's autumns and winters comprise days of leaden skies and sparse sunshine, which are not the best conditions for taking photographs. That said there are some distinctive shots (beside the obvious one of the Brandenburg Gate, which fills a photo frame nicely) that keen photographers can aim for that define the city: old/new contrasts can be very striking, for example, the juxtaposition of the medieval Mariankirche and the space-age TV Tower (Fersehturm; see page 72), or the bombed-out spire of the nineteenth century Kaiser-Wilhelm-Gedächtniskirche church (see page 38) which contrasts with the distinctive 1960s rebuilt church and tower on either side. Artwork on the remaining stretches of the Berlin Wall in the East Side Gallery (see page 75) can also allow for photos that are unique to the city. Finally, a sunny day in summer photographing some of the luxurious Baroque palaces in Potsdam (see page 87) or the Schloss Charlottenburg (see page 76), both of which are set in formal gardens, will make up for the distinct lack of similar opportunities in the city centre.

city's post-war rebirth; the latter has walls comprising stained glass made in Chartres set in moulded concrete, and casts a mysterious bluish glow over the Ku'damm at night.

What remains of this neo-Romanesque church (originally built between 1891 and 1895 to honour Wilhelm I) now constitutes a memorial hall to celebrate the Hohenzollerns' pious monarchism and the rebirth of the church after war. A mosaic representing

Christ the King is set above friezes and reliefs of Prussian monarchs from Friedrich I (1415–40) to the last crown prince, Friedrich Wilhelm. With their taste for irreverent nicknames, Berliners have deflated the monuments' imperial or pacifist intentions by dubbing the original church the 'hollow tooth' and the two main additions the 'lipstick' and 'powder compact'.

Immediately east of the church and fountain is the enormous **Europa-Center** (https://europa-center-berlin.de) between Tauentzienstraße and Budapester Straße. The centre was built in the 1960s and houses scores of shops, restaurants, a gameshow experience known as the SpieleArena and a cabaret theatre amid artificial ponds and waterfalls.

The Zoo

Accessed from Budapester Straße, the **Berlin Zoo** ❹ (www.zoo-berlin.de; charge, with extra cost for aquarium), is Germany's oldest (opened 1844) and is the most visited in Europe, with one of the most varied collections of animals on the continent. Beyond the pagoda-arched **Elefantentor** (Elephant Gate) are 35 hectares (86 acres) of parkland where you can observe Indian and African elephants, giant pandas and the rare Indian single-horned rhinoceros. Dating from 1913, the **Zoo-Aquarium Berlin** houses numerous species of fish and reptiles..

Tauentzienstraße

From Breidscheidplatz, follow the double-laned **Tauentzienstraße** to the east. In the pleasantly landscaped central reservation, notice the intertwined steel tubes of the ***Berlin*** sculpture ❺, which was designed

NOTES

A good initial way of getting the measure of Berlin is to take the S-Bahn around the centre, from Zoologischer Garten to Alexanderplatz. From the elevated track, you get impressive views of major landmarks, including the Reichstag.

for the city's 750th anniversary in 1987. The two halves are tantalisingly close to each other, yet fail to touch, poignantly symbolising the once divided city.

Entrance to the Berlin Zoo

Wittenbergplatz

At the far end of Tauentzienstraße, **Wittenbergplatz** is a large, busy square containing one of Berlin's many memorials: it takes the form of a stark sign outside the U-Bahn station that lists Nazi concentration camps as simply if they were on the schedule of daily commuter trains. The sign is a reminder of exactly what happened when Jews were rounded up and deported in Berlin and hundreds of other towns and cities: their neighbours hardly reacted, just as the many commuters and visitors who use the station today hardly react to the sign as they hurry past it. The station itself is a beautifully restored Art Deco delight with lovely wooden ticket booths, period posters and a central standing clock.

More than just a department store, **KaDeWe** (Kaufhaus des Westens; www.kadewe.de), located on the edge of Wittenbergplatz, has been a city institution since its foundation in 1907. The food emporium on the sixth floor is extraordinary. Here, gourmets can perch on a bar stool and sample food from around the world – there are bars and eateries serving everything from caviar to pizza, and the quantity of sweets, chocolate and wine on sale is quite eye-opening. One floor up, the Wintergarten is a vast food court in the glass-roofed atrium where shoppers can help themselves to more scrumptious fare. It is an ideal spot for a hearty breakfast before a day's shopping. The fashion department (spread across three floors) is also well worth a visit.

Tiergarten Area

Highlights

- **Hansaviertel**, see page 43
- **Siegessäule**, see page 44
- **Haus der Kulturen der Welt**, see page 44
- **The Reichstag**, see page 45
- **Contemporary Art and Natural History museums**, see page 46
- **Berlin Wall Memorial and Dokumentationszentrum**, see page 47
- **Bauhaus Archiv building**, see page 47
- **Stauffenbergstraße**, see page 48
- **Kulturforum**, see page 49
- **Neue Nationalgalerie and Berlin Modern**, see page 51
- **Potsdamer Platz**, see page 52
- **South of Potsdamer Platz**, see page 54

Despite its name, the leafy **Tiergarten** (literally 'animal garden') is not another zoo. For the Hohenzollern princes, it was a forest for hunting deer and wild boar. Frederick the Great cut down the woods to create a formal French garden for his brother August Ferdinand, but it was replanted with trees in the nineteenth century and transformed into a landscaped park. Following World War II, Berliners stripped away the trees again, this time for fuel.

Within the park, the **Englischer Garten** (24-hour access; free) was laid out after the war with 5,000 tree donations from the gardens of George VI and UK citizens; it was opened by foreign secretary Sir

Anthony Eden in 1952 (and for a long time was known by Berliners as The Garden of Eden). It forms part of the grounds of the neoclassical **Schloss Bellevue**, the official residence of the German president. The building is visible from the street, but not surprisingly is inaccessible to the public.

The Haus der Kulturen der Welt

In the far northeast of the park, close to the Brandenburg Gate, the **Soviet War Memorial** (Sowjetisches Ehrenmal) commemorates the Red Army troops who died in the battle for Berlin. It was built very soon after the capitulation of Germany in 1945, using marble from Hitler's ruined Reich Chancellery, and is flanked by the two tanks that were the first to reach the city. In Cold War days, it was marooned in West Berlin, though it still had a Soviet guard of honour; today it is maintained by the City of Berlin.

Hansaviertel

On the northwest side of the Tiergarten is the **Hansaviertel**, a residential neighbourhood rebuilt by architects for the International Building Exhibition of 1957. Among the winners were Bauhaus founder Walter Gropius and the Brazilian Oscar Niemeyer. Their constructions, clustered around the southern exit of Hansaplatz U-Bahn, remain a striking assemblage to this day. Nearby, at Hanseatenweg 10, the **Akademie der Künste** (Arts Academy;

https://adk.de/; charge), distinguished by the splendid Henry Moore sculpture outside, holds concerts, plays and exhibitions of contemporary art and photography.

Siegessäule

At the centre of the park is the Großer Stern, a large traffic circle at whose centre is the soaring **Siegessäule** (Victory Column; www.siegessaeule-berlin.de/; charge), an unabashed monument to Prussian militarism. It was completed in 1873, two years after the victory over the French, and also marks successes against Denmark (1864) and Austria (1866). Access to the monument is via the tunnels under the circling traffic lanes; after viewing an exhibition about its construction, there's a climb of around 285 steps to reach the top of the 67m (220ft) column for a breathtaking view of the city. Monuments around the Großer Stern honour the architects of the unification of Germany.

Haus der Kulturen der Welt

Follow the River Spree to the east along Spreeweg until you reach the former **Kongreßhalle**, built by the Americans as their contribution to the 1957 International Building Exhibition. Officially renamed **Haus der Kulturen der Welt** (House of World Cultures; www.hkw.de/), the striking design, with its curved concrete roof, led Berliners to dub the building the 'pregnant oyster'. The venue hosts art exhibitions, concerts, films, conferences, speaker meetings and art exhibitions, with a focus on non-European cultures and societies. In front of the building, the pond features a sculpture by Henry Moore (*Large Divided Oval: Butterfly*, made in 1986 and his heaviest sculpture in bronze), which is attractively illuminated at night. An austere black structure stands on the corner of Große Querallee near the Kongreßhalle. Built in 1987, the 42m (138ft) tall tower contains a 68-bell **carillon**, which chimes daily at noon and 6pm.

The Reichstag

A few minutes' walk eastwards from the Haus der Kulturen der Welt, you will find the **Reichstag** ❻ building (S-Bahn Friedrichstraße; www.bundestag.de), its huge glass dome, with its mirrored central funnel, visible from much of the city and symbolic of a new Germany that keeps no secrets from its people. The parliamentary home of Wilhelminian and Weimar Germany displays the proud dedication *Dem deutschen Volke* (To the German People) on a Neoclassical façade built in 1894 by Paul Wallot. This appeal to patriotism and democracy, set above six Corinthian columns, outlasted the burning in 1933 and the bombs of World War II, and was given renewed significance when Berlin resumed its former role as the seat of government of a unified Germany. Today, the dome, designed by Sir Norman Foster, is a major attraction for Berliners and tourists alike. They endure lengthy queues to be able to travel to the top, gazing out at the city from the rooftop terrace and down into the Bundestag chamber. To join them, you must first register online (www.bundestag.de/en/visittheBundestag/dome/registration-245686; free).

The Reichstag now forms the centrepiece of what is otherwise a completely modern government quarter. To the immediate north of the Reichstag is an impressive

Berlin Victory Column

complex of buildings designed by Stefan Braunfels: the **Paul-Löbe-Haus** houses the committee rooms of the Bundestag and parliamentarians' offices.

Take a stroll east along **Paul-Löbe-Allee**, which runs between the **Reichstag** and **Paul-Löbe-Haus**, and you'll reach the **promenade** along the river's south bank that links the Reichstag and Friedrichstraße station. Where the promenade begins, close to the Reichstag's Northeast corner, there are three features to look out for: a metal memorial with white crosses on a black background, erected in honour of eight East Germans killed while attempting to flee to the West (the river here formed the border); a section of brick wall from the Gdansk shipyard in Poland, which the Solidarity Trade Union leader Lech Wałęsa climbed over in 1980 to proclaim the workers' strike that led to the fall of communism; and a little further on, a sculpture representing the Berlin Wall – behind glass panelling with paragraphs of the German Constitution etched into it.

The Reichstag dome

Contemporary Art and Natural History museums

Easily reached from the Reichstag via one of the Spree bridges, and within easy reach of the impressive Hauptbahnhof, are Invalidenstraße and two of Berlin's most fascinating museums. A splendid example of early railway architecture, the elegant old Hamburger Bahnhof is now the **Museum of Contemporary Art** (www.smb.museum/en; charge), a spacious setting for works by modern masters like Joseph Beuys and Andy Warhol. The works here are all post-1960, and there's a focus on video installations and photography. Another venerable building, the 100-year-old **Museum für Naturkunde** ❼ (Natural History Museum; www.museumfuernaturkunde.berlin/de; charge) is one of the finest of its kind, with some 25 million objects in its collections.

Berlin Wall Memorial and Dokumentationszentrum

Six hundred metres to the east of the Natural History Museum, the area stretching along Bernauerstrasse from Nordbahnhof S-Bahn station provides a fascinating outdoor memorial and museum of the Berlin Wall. In the station itself there's an exhibition about how the East German authorities attempted to thwart escapees heading for the West via U-Bahn tunnels; across the road from the station is a visitor centre with bookshop and documentary films to watch about the Wall (free); along Bernauerstrasse parts of the wall (and a watchtower) have been preserved, alongside various monuments commemorating the residential blocks and the church that were demolished to make way for the Wall (the latter has been replaced by a strikingly modern church positioned right on the former 'death strip'); and the Wall's history is outlined in the Dokumentationszentrum Berliner Mauer (https://stiftung-berliner-mauer.de/de/gedenkstaette-berliner-mauer; free) on Bernauerstrasse, where you can climb up to a viewing platform that looks out over the whole site.

Bauhaus Archiv building

Back near the Tiergarten, south of the Siegessäule at the corner of Stülerstraße and Klingelhöferstraße, stands the elegant, modern, shared complex that houses the **Embassies of the Nordic Countries** (Denmark, Finland, Norway, Sweden and Iceland). Completed in 1999, the architecture is a stunning showcase for Scandinavian design and materials.

On Klingelhöferstraße the new Bauhaus Archive/Museum für Gestaltung (www.bauhaus.de) should open during the lifetime of this guide, replacing the temporary museum on Knesebeckstraße. The museum documents the hugely influential achievements of the Bauhaus, the most progressive early twentieth-century institution of its kind. Architects like Walter Gropius, Mies van der Rohe and Marcel Breuer collaborated with artists such as Paul Klee, Vasili Kandinsky, Lyonel Feininger, Oskar Schlemmer and Laszlo Moholy-Nagy, in an attempt to integrate arts, crafts and architecture into mass industrial society. On view here is a selection of the objects they created: tubular steel chairs, cups and saucers, teapots, desks, new weaves for carpets, chess pieces and children's building blocks, as well as some pioneering architectural plans and sketches.

Stauffenbergstraße

Follow the north bank of the tree-lined Landwehrkanal along the Reichpietschufer as far as Stauffenbergstraße. On the corner stands one of Berlin's most striking works of Modernist architecture, the **Gasag Building** (or Shell Haus), designed by Emil Fahrenkamp and built for Shell Oil in 1930. This was one of the first steel-framed high-rise buildings in Berlin. Its flowing curves, lightness of style and use of glass provide a stark contrast to the Nazi architecture built later in the 1930s, as seen, for example, in the Japanese Embassy on nearby Hildebrandstraße, or indeed at the next attraction. The **Gedenkstätte Deutscher Widerstand** (www.gdw-berlin.de; free) at Stauffenbergstraße 13–14 (opposite the Marriott Hotel) is a memorial to German resistance against the Nazi regime. It's located within the *Bendlerblock*, an enormous building constructed just before World War I as the Headquarters of the German Navy, and today still in the hands of the country's Ministry of Defence. A bronze statue depicting a young man with bound hands stands in the courtyard where Graf von Stauffenberg, and other army officers who conspired to blow up Hitler on 20 July 1944, were shot (in 2008 permission was given for the execution scene from the Tom Cruise film *Valkyrie*, which tells the story of the plot, to be filmed here). An excellent exhibition, in the rooms of the building where the attempted coup was planned, charts the tragic course of resistance – not only von Staufenberg's but also of others who bravely defied the Nazis, including those who helped hide and support Jewish people.

The Modernist Gasag building

Follow Stauffenbergstraße to its junction with Tiergartenstraße. At the corner is the **Austrian Embassy**. Designed by Austrian architect Hans Hollein and completed in 2001, its three distinct parts, rendered in green, orange and grey, reflect the different functions within the building. The embassy marks the eastern gateway to the diplomatic quarter, which runs along Tiergartenstraße to the left. In the other direction, Tiergartenstraße leads straight to the Kulturforum.

Kulturforum

Situated just west of Potsdamer Platz, the **Kulturforum** (S-Bahn/U-Bahn Potsdamer Platz) is a complex of concert halls and museums built on land levelled first by the plans of Albert Speer, Hitler's architect, to redesign the city, and then by the bombs of World War II. It is clustered around the only building to survive from previous eras, the **Matthäikirche**, which was built in the neo-Romanesque style in 1846 by August Stüler and stands in dignified isolation on Matthäikirchplatz.

The quality of exhibits in the museums here is outstanding (information for all can be found at www.smb.museum; charges for each museum). Completed in 1998, the **Gemäldegalerie** ❽ is home to a remarkable collection of German, Dutch, Flemish, French, English, Spanish and Italian paintings from the thirteenth to the eighteenth centuries. Among the works are masterpieces such as Hans Holbein's *Portrait of the Merchant Georg Gisze* (1532); *The Fountain of Youth* (1546) by Lucas Cranach the Elder, which is an amusing commentary on the search for eternal youth; and Vermeer's study *Young Lady with a Pearl Necklace* (1644). Other artists represented include Peter Paul Rubens, Titian, Botticelli and Caravaggio.

Adjacent to the gallery, the **Kunstgewerbemuseum** displays a wide range of the most exquisitely executed arts and crafts, from medieval times to the present day, with gold and silversmith work, glass, enamel and porcelain vessels, furniture, room panelling, tapestries and costumes on display. Among its treasures is the Engerer Burse, a reliquary from Enger Abbey that takes the form of a bag made from gold sheets set with precious stones, which was made around AD 780 and is considered one of the most important examples of Carolingian goldsmith work.

The **Kupferstichkabinett** (Prints and Drawings Collection) is one of the world's finest graphics collections, with works ranging from fourteenth-century illuminated manuscripts to modern woodcuts by Erich Heckel and lithographs by Willem de Kooning. Also on display are outstanding works from Dürer and Botticelli through Rembrandt to Picasso and Andy Warhol.

The Merchant Georg Gisze by Hans Holbein the Younger

The architect Hans Scharoun is famous for his Expressionistic free-form structures. His first design, the controversial ochre and gold **Philharmonie** ❾ (www.berliner-philharmoniker.de), owes its tent-like shape to the demands of the concert hall's acoustics and sight-lines. The home of the Berlin Philharmonic Orchestra was designed from the inside out, from the orchestra to the walls and roof. Viewed from across Tiergartenstraße, the nearby **Musikinstrumentenmuseum** (www.sim.spk-berlin.de; charge), also by Scharoun, is reminiscent of an open card index file. Its extensive collection of instruments from the sixteenth century to the present day includes a 1703 Stradivarius violin, the 1810 piano of composer Carl Maria von Weber, and a 1929 New York Wurlitzer cinema organ, which comes alive in concerts. The website gives details of tours of the museum (usually twice weekly) and of the concerts on the Wurlitzer organ (usually weekly).

Neue Nationalgalerie and Berlin Modern

Just south of the Matthäikirche at the corner of Potsdamer Straße is the **Neue Nationalgalerie** ❿ (www.smb.museum/museen-einrichtungen/neue-nationalgalerie/home). This square, glass-wall structure with its vast, black steel roof supported by eight massive steel columns, was designed by Bauhaus master Mies van der Rohe and completed in 1968, a year before his death. The building is of characteristic elegant simplicity and is considered a prime example of structural abstraction emblematic of the International Style. It stands on a raised granite platform that serves as a sculpture court for huge pieces like Henry Moore's *Archer*. Next door is its new extension, Berlin Modern, designed by the Swiss architectural firm Herzog & de Meuron; construction work began on this €450m project in 2019, and it will open during the lifetime of this guide. The primary focus of the gallery is twentieth-century art, with Cubism, Expressionism, the Bauhaus, and Surrealism particularly represented through artists such as Pablo Picasso, Ernst Ludwig Kirchner, Joan Miró, Wassily Kandinsky and Barnett Newman.

Potsdamer Platz

Reduced by war and the Wall to a bleak no-man's land, **Potsdamer Platz ⓫**, the square that was at one time the busiest in Europe,

ANHALTER BAHNHOF

Anhalter Bahnhof was once Berlin's most glamorous railway station, linking the city to Europe's other great capitals. It's westbound platform staged the tragic last act of the Weimar Republic: soon after Hitler became chancellor, Berlin's most gifted artists and intellectuals – among them Heinrich Mann, Bertolt Brecht, Kurt Weill, Georg Grosz and Albert Einstein – gathered here, their bags packed for the 'last train to freedom'. The station was patched up after the war, but after the border was sealed, it stood at the end of a line to nowhere and became redundant. Today, all that remains of Anhalter Bahnhof is the restored entrance portico to the main hall; the land on which the station itself once stood is covered by playing fields and Berlin's tent-like Tempodrom events venue.

has burst back into life in the most bracing fashion. What was once a scar on the landscape, epitomising the division of the city and country, is now a thriving arts, entertainment, shopping and business centre. The impact of the towering, modern buildings, made predominantly from glass, is astounding. Investment from corporations such as Daimler-Chrysler and Sony has resulted in the construction of shopping malls, a theatre, a casino and some great hotels.

Berliner Philharmonie

Almost 100,000 people arrive here daily to marvel at the striking architecture and explore the latest attractions in this city-within-a-city. The Center Potsdamer Platz (known as the Sony Center until 2023) is an entertainment complex, contained within a central courtyard under a glass ceiling; it is also home to the Legoland Discovery Centre Berlin (www.legolanddiscoverycentre.com/berlin/en/). Immediately to the south, across the road from the semicircular Bahn Tower (the HQ of Deutsche Bahn), the Kohlhoff Tower is worth a visit for its **Panoramapunkt** viewing platform (Potsdamer Platz 1; www.panoramapunkt.de; charge), offering a grand view of central Berlin (and reached by what is allegedly Europe's fastest lift).

Situated to the immediate north of the Center Potsdamer Platz, the eighteen-storey **Beisheim Center**, housing the Ritz Carlton

NOTES

A poignant contrast to the futuristic architecture and technological content of the Center Potsdamer Platz can be found in the elegant remains of the old Grandhotel Esplanade, now preserved behind glass walls at the eastern entrance. Before it was almost completely destroyed during World War II, the hotel was a meeting point for the international rich and famous, including stars such as Greta Garbo and Charlie Chaplin.

Hotel, and the seventeen-storey **Delbrück-Haus**, provide a skyline reminiscent of Art Deco skyscrapers in New York and Chicago. Stretching away to the south, the Arkaden shopping centre became a firm favourite with city shoppers as soon as it opened in 1998, and the cafés, casino and theatres in Marlene-Dietrich-Platz are equally popular.

South of Potsdamer Platz

The **Martin-Gropius-Bau** (commonly known as the Gropius Bau; www.berlinerfestspiele.de/en/gropius-bau/ueber-uns/ueber-den-gropius-bau), situated nearby at Stresemann Straße 110, was originally built as an arts and crafts museum. Erected between 1877 and 1881 by Martin Gropius (great-uncle of the Bauhaus's Walter Gropius), with the help of Heino Schmieden, the lavish red and gold building is now a venue for exhibitions, concerts and stage productions. Art and architecture exhibits are displayed in and around its skylighted inner courtyard area.

Adjacent to the Martin-Gropius-Bau is the site of Prinz-Albrecht-Straße 8, the building that served as the headquarters of the SS, Gestapo and other Nazi institutions. Excavations in 1987 revealed cellars where thousands of victims were imprisoned and tortured.

The building constructed above the former Gestapo and SS headquarters houses the **Topographie des Terrors** ⓬ (www.topographie.de; free), an outdoor and indoor museum that illustrates the persecution of those who resisted the Nazi terror. Berlin has many reminders of its dark past, but this place has a particular impact. A section of the Berlin Wall remains in place next to the site.

Further along at Askanischer Platz is the restored ruin of the entrance portico of **Anhalter Bahnhof** (see page 52). The old railway station was the work of Franz Schwechten, the architect who designed that other noble ruin, the Kaiser Wilhelm Memorial Church (see page 28).

You can't miss the **Deutsches Technikmuseum Berlin** ⓭ (U-Bahn Gleisdreieck, S-Bahn Anhalter Bahnhof; https://technikmuseum.berlin) on the banks of the Landwehrkanal: poised over its entrance is the front end of one of the original transport planes from the Berlin Airlift, a Douglas DC3. Built over the freight yards of the Anhalter Bahnhof, this is one of the city's most fascinating museums, with exhibits dealing with all aspects of transport and technology, from railways, aviation, shipping and road transport to textiles, medicine, communications and printing. In the engineering section, you can get hands on and use various bits of machinery and participate in experiments.

A touch of New York or Chicago at Potsdamer Platz

On and around Unter Den Linden

Highlights

The area east of the Brandenburg Gate, known as Mitte (Middle), is the historic centre of Berlin and was once the centre of the capital of the German Democratic Republic (GDR). The city's most important museums, government buildings, churches and theatres were constructed here in the eighteenth, nineteenth and twentieth centuries. Many buildings were restored by the GDR after Allied bombing in World War II, and several quarters were almost completely rebuilt in their old style, notably Gendarmenmarkt and Museumsinsel (see pages 61 and 65). Post reunification, restoration continued apace, façades returned to their former glory, and some striking new additions were made by internationally acclaimed architects. Today, the area's principal avenue, **Unter den Linden**, has regained its former importance as the main focus of the capital's cultural and political life, while nearby Friedrichstraße is once again Berlin's fashionable shopping artery lined with high-end designer boutiques and department stores.

Brandenburg Gate

Deutsches Technikmuseum

This formidable symbol of the united city appears at last to be realising the vision of Johann Gottfried Schadow, the sculptor who crowned the **Brandenburger Tor** ⓮ with the Quadriga, a copper statue of Winged Victory in her four-horse chariot (the one you see today is a copy, after the original was damaged in the War). Schadow had wanted the gate to be known as the *Friedenstor* (Gate of Peace), in keeping with the relief of the *Procession of Peace* that he had sculpted beneath Victory's simple chariot. But in former time the gate was the venue for military parades – Napoleon and the Nazis staged them here – and then during the days of the Berlin Wall it was isolated as part of the defensive 'Death Strip' and accessible to no-one. But nowadays, locals on their morning run just nonchalantly jog through it, and the 'Gate of Peace' moniker seems appropriate.

The gate itself, designed by Carl Gotthard Langhans, was built between 1789 and 1791. With two rows of six Doric columns forming the gateway proper, it was inspired by the Propylaeum gatehouse leading to the Parthenon in Athens. Forming part of the city wall, the gate was intended by the pragmatic Prussians not so much as a triumphal arch as an imposing tollgate for collecting duties.

Brandenburg Gate

After decades of inaccessibility when the Wall came down, the gate subsequently became the scene of quite ecstatic celebrations when it came down. Today, in deference to Johann Gottfried Schadow's original vision, the north wing of the gate houses a 'quiet room' where visitors are invited to sit and contemplate in peace; the south wing houses a tourist information centre.

Pariser Platz

In front of the Brandenburg Gate is the cobbled Pariser Platz, an expansive square surrounded by buildings of varying styles; it's one of Berlin's great gathering points for tourists, though because of the nearby presence of the American, British, Russian and French embassies they have to share the space with a fairly hefty police presence.

On the right, looking east, the square is dominated by the smartest hotel in town, the supremely elegant **Hotel Adlon Kempinski**, rebuilt on the site of the original Hotel Adlon, a 1920s Berlin legend. On the square at the side of the Adlon is the glass façade of the **Akademie der Künste** (https://adk.de/; charge), designed by Günter Behnisch and with a changing programme of art and photography exhibitions. Next to that, the **DZ Bank** building designed by Californian architect Frank Gehry gives little clue as to what lies inside – a remarkable atrium covered by a vaulted glass roof said to have the form of a fish, beneath which a walk-in sculpture resembling Captain Nemo's *Nautilus* is in fact the outer skin of a conference room. Visitors can go in, but no further than the entrance hall's security turnstiles. Sandwiched between the bank and the Brandenburg Gate is the **US Embassy**, with the French Embassy facing it across the square.

Unter den Linden to Friedrichstraße

Sweeping eastwards from Pariser Platz, the grand 61m (200ft) wide avenue, literally named 'Beneath the Linden Trees', was Berlin's showcase boulevard. Frederick the Great saw it as the centre of his royal capital, and it became the most prestigious address in town. Some of its splendour fell victim to nineteenth-century building speculation, but the avenue remained fashionable until the bombs of World War II reduced it to rubble. Now the trees have been replanted and most of the important buildings have finally been restored.

A short distance down on the right is Wilhelmstraße (again with a notable police presence and blocked off to cars). Until World War II, this was where the British Embassy was situated, as was the Reichspräsidentenpalais (Palace of the President of the Reich), the Foreign Office, the Reichskanzlei (Chancellery), as well as many other ministries. The **British Embassy** is here once again, housed in a striking modern building (Nos 70/71) designed by Michael

Holocaust Memorial

Wilford and Partners and officially opened by the Queen in July 2000.

Holocaust Memorial

A right turn off Wilhelmstraße leads to the **Holocaust Memorial** (www.stiftung-denkmal.de), which runs south along Friedrich-Ebert-Straße in the direction of Potsdamer Platz. New York architect Peter Eisenman's concept is deliberately disorientating; an extensive area of ground planted with 2,700 concrete pillars of differing heights and no designated entrance or exit. There is an information centre underneath, though security searches are made, and you may have to queue to get in. It's best to arrive early if you want to visit.

Madame Tussauds and Friedrichstraße

Back on Unter den Linden, Berlin's branch of **Madame Tussauds** (www.madametussauds.com; charge) is on the street's north side; here you can rub shoulders with the likes of Bismarck, Lionel Messi, Karl Marx and Angela Merkel – and there's even free entry for those who can prove (via photo ID) that it's their birthday! A little further down on the right is the **Embassy of the Russian Federation**. As with the British embassy, the site has a long history of being a venue for international diplomacy, dating in this case back to 1832 when Tsar Nicholas II opened the Russian Embassy to the

German Empire here. The current building dates from 1952 and is very Soviet in style.

About halfway along, Friedrichstraße crosses Unter den Linden. Much new building work was completed along this famous street in the early part of the Noughties, both to the north, where Friedrichstraße has been restored, and to the south, where architectural monstrosities built during the days of the GDR have been demolished and replaced by a very elegant development of designer shops, offices and apartments.

Gendarmenmarkt

From Friedrichstraße, follow Jägerstraße or Taubenstraße to reach **Gendarmenmarkt** ⓱, the celebrated architectural ensemble south of Unter den Linden. This grand square, bordered by bookshops and cafés set in delightful arcades, has been almost completely restored after being blasted to smithereens during World War II. The imposing **Schiller-Denkmal** (1868), a monument sculpted in Carrara marble, surrounds a statue of the writer Friedrich von Schiller with the muses of philosophy, poetry, drama and history. It stands in front of Schinkel's Ionic-porticoed **Konzerthaus**. Originally called the Schauspielhaus (Playhouse), this is now a concert hall. It stands between two identical churches, the **Französischer Dom** (or French Cathedral) to the north, built for the immigrant Huguenots, and the **Deutscher Dom** (German Cathedral) to the south. Both were built in the early eighteenth century. The domes were added in 1785.

Step inside the Französischer Dom to visit the **Hugenottenmuseum** (https://hugenottenmuseum-berlin.de/; charge) and to climb the stairwell inside the bell tower to reach a viewing platform with predictably panoramic views. The Deutscher Dom houses a free exhibition about Germany's recent social and political history, cleverly combining documents, photographs and radio broadcasts to chronicle the rise of Nazism and the development of democracy. Unfortunately, there's little information in English, and the exhibition is recommended for German speakers who have an interest in the country's parliamentary history, in particular.

Checkpoint Charlie

Towards the southern end of Friedrichstraße is the site of **Checkpoint Charlie**, that infamous border crossing between East and West. Six weeks after the building of the Wall, it was here that American and Russian tanks faced each other in what was one of the tensest stand-offs of the Cold War. Today, the barbed wire and barriers are gone, but the memories remain. Next to the reconstructed US army checkpoint hut and the famous sign that proclaims 'You are now leaving the American sector' (actually a replica), the **Haus am Checkpoint Charlie** ⓯ (U-Bahn Kochstraße; www.mauermuseum.de; charge) celebrates the ingenuity and courage of those who sought to escape to the West, and commemorates those who died doing so. Very close by is another exhibition, Blackbox Cold War (https://blackbox-kalter-krieg.de/; charge) which covers some of the same ground as the Wall Museum though looks more at the Cold War in general; and the Asisi Panorama (www.die-mauer.de/), an enormous panorama by artist Yadegar Asisi that depicts a normal day in Berlin when the Berlin Wall was up and the Kreuzberg district was a favourite with punks and squatters.

NOTES

Sections of the wall can prove hard to track down in today's Berlin. A good idea is to go on the Berlin Wall Bike Tour and ride alongside the wall's former location with a knowledgeable English-speaking guide. The 15km (9-mile) tour lasts roughly 3.5 hours and runs from March to early November. For more information, visit www.berlinonbike.de.

The Film Museum and the Jewish Museum

Some 250m to the Northwest of Checkpoint Charlie,

housed in a 1920s electricity substation at Mauerstraße 79, is the **Film Museum Berlin** (www.deutsche-kinemathek.de). This absorbing museum commemorates the city's history in cinema production and pays tribute to the greatest of German screen stars, Marlene Dietrich.

Memories of human tragedy on a scale even wider than the Berlin Wall can be found at the **Jüdisches Museum** ⓰ (U-Bahn Hallesches Tor; www.jmberlin.de; charge), south of Checkpoint Charlie on Lindenstraße. With its jagged outline and its disorientating interior of sloping galleries and unexpected angles, Daniel Libeskind's striking zinc-faced building symbolises the troubled course of Jewish life in Germany and the devastation of the Holocaust. Its exhibits give a comprehensive and moving account.

The British Embassy

Unter den Linden to Schlossbrücke

East of Charlottenstraße is the patched, dark stone of the **Deutsche Staatsbibliothek** (German State Library), the former Prussian State Library, built between 1903 and 1914 but damaged during World War II; it's now the research division of the Berlin State Library. Adjacent is the **Humboldt Universität.** The main building was erected between 1748–66 by Johann Boumann as a palace for Prince Heinrich, the brother of Frederick II. In 1810, on the initiative

Checkpoint Charlie

of the eminent scientists Alexander and Wilhelm von Humboldt, it was converted to a seat of learning. At this point, an imposing **statue of Frederick the Great on Horseback** (1851), by Christian Daniel Rauch, stands in the avenue's central strip.

Heinrich's Palace was just part of a grand scheme commissioned by Frederick the Great to recreate the cultural climate that his grandfather had brought to Berlin during the seventeenth century. Known as the Forum Fridericianum, the major portion of the scheme occupies the other side of Unter den Linden around the open square called **Bebelplatz** (formerly Opernplatz), which was the scene of book-burning by Nazi students in 1933. On the west side is the curving Baroque façade of the **Alte Bibliothek** (Old Library). Facing it to the east is the grand Palladian-style **Staatsoper Unter den Linden** (State Opera), designed in 1742 by von Knobelsdorff, Frederick the Great's favourite architect. To the south of the Staatsoper on the corner of Bebelplatz is **St Hedwigs-Kathedrale**, a huge, domed structure built for the Catholics incorporated into Protestant Prussia by Frederick's conquest of Silesia.

Beside the university, the **Neue Wache** ⓲ (New Guardhouse; free) was Karl Friedrich Schinkel's first important building, completed in 1818. After serving as the GDR's 'Memorial to the Victims of Fascism and Militarism', the little neoclassical structure that resembles a Roman temple now commemorates all victims of war and tyranny. Inside is a large copy of Käthe Kollwitz's poignant *Grieving Mother* sculpture and a granite slab covering the tombs of an unknown soldier and a Concentration Camp victim.

Next door is the handsome, Baroque **Zeughaus**, once an arsenal for the Prussian Army, as the sculpted suits of armour along the roof testify. The artist Andreas Schlüter (see box, page 67) provided the military sculpture, but was able to assert more pacifistic views with poignant sculpted masks of dying warriors (1696) in the inner courtyard named after him, the **Schlüterhof**.

Now splendidly restored and with a glittering annexe by the American architect I.M. Pei, the Zeughaus is the home of the **Deutsches Historisches Museum** (www.dhm.de; charge), with rich collections on national history.

Linking Unter den Linden to Karl-Liebknecht-Straße is the exquisite **Schlossbrücke** ⓳ (Palace Bridge), designed by Schinkel in 1820–24, but built after he died in the 1850s, and adorned with fierce warriors and victory goddesses.

Museum Island

Beyond the bridge, the imposing contemporary façade of the James-Simon-Galerie, visible over to the left behind the Altes Museum, forms both the main entrance and the visitor centre for the **Museumsinsel** (Museum Island; www.smb.museum/en/museums-institutions/museumsinsel-berlin/home; U-Bahn/S-Bahn Friedrichstraße, S-Bahn Hackescher Markt), the site

NOTES

Among the renowned academics to work at the Humboldt University were the philosophers Hegel and Schleiermacher, philologists Jacob and Wilhelm Grimm, physicists Max Planck, Albert Einstein and Otto Hahn and physicians Virchow, Koch and Sauerbruch.

The Neue Wache, built by Karl Friedrich Schinkel

of Berlin's most important museums. The gallery, opened in 2019, has information and ticket desks, a café, a gift shop, lecture auditoriums and special exhibition spaces, and provides direct access to some of the museums.

The **Altes Museum** is a fine neoclassical building, generally regarded as Schinkel's masterpiece. The massive polished granite bowl in front was originally intended to sit atop the edifice. The museum houses an astonishing collection of Greek and Roman antiquities, including vases, statues, sarcophagi and funerary goods.

Beyond Bodestraße is the **Alte Nationalgalerie**, a temple to nineteenth-century art. Rooms on the upper floor house a fine collection of works by Romantic painters; the 24 paintings by Caspar David Friedrich here constitute the largest number of works by him under one roof. Among them, look for *Abtei im Eichwald*

The U- and S-Bahn

MINI
BERLIN

First Edition 2025

Editor: Beth Williams
Author: Andrew Beattie
Picture Editor: Piotr Kala
Picture Manager: Tom Smyth
Cartography Update: Katie Bennett
Layout: Danielle Titmas
Production Operations Manager: Katie Bennett
Publishing Technology Manager: Rebeka Davies
Head of Publishing: Sarah Clark
Photography Credits: Dreamstime 77; iStock 6, 14TL, 14BL, 14BR, 15T, 15B, 23, 25, 37, 38, 41, 46, 55, 58, 60, 64, 69, 74, 80, 82, 88, 113; Max Lautenschläger/Staatsoper Unter den Linden 94; Public domain 26, 51; Shutterstock 1, 9, 11, 13, 14TR 14CL, 14CR, 15CT, 15CB, 16T, 16CL, 16BL, 16BR, 18T, 18CL, 18BR, 18BL, 20T, 20CL, 20BR, 20BL, 29, 31, 32, 34, 43, 45, 49, 53, 57, 63, 66, 70, 73, 79, 84, 86, 90, 92, 97, 99, 100, 103, 104, 109, 110, 114
Cover Credits: U-Bahn train on the Oberbaum Bridge **Leo Patrizi/iStock**

About the author
Andrew Beattie studied geography at Oxford University and has been writing and travelling ever since. He has worked on books in the Rough Guides series on Syria, Switzerland, Germany, Europe on a Budget and the Lake Geneva region, and has written a number of cultural guides (published by Signal Books) to the Scottish Highlands, the River Danube, the Alps, Cairo and Prague. Home (when he's not travelling) is in Southeast London.

Distribution
UK, Ireland and Europe: Apa Publications (UK) Ltd; mail@roughguides.com
United States and Canada: Two Rivers; ips@ingramcontent.com
Australia and New Zealand: Woodslane; info@woodslane.com.au
Worldwide: Apa Publications (UK) Ltd; mail@roughguides.com

MIX
Paper from responsible sources
FSC® C014138

Special Sales, Content Licensing and CoPublishing
Rough Guides can be purchased in bulk quantities at discounted prices. We can create special editions, personalized jackets and corporate imprints tailored to your needs.
mail@roughguides.com
roughguides.com

EU Representative
LOGOS EUROPE, 9 rue Nicolas Poussin, 17000, LA ROCHELLE, France; Contact@logoseurope.eu; +33 (0) 667937378

Printed by Finidr in Czech Republic

ISBN: 9781835292488

This book was produced using **Typefi** automated publishing software.

A catalogue record for this book is available from the British Library

Contact us
Every effort has been made to ensure that this publication is accurate, free from safety risks, and provides accurate information. However, changes and errors are inevitable. The publisher is not responsible for any resulting loss, inconvenience, injury or safety concerns arising from the use of this book. If you notice any errors, outdated information, or potential safety risks, please send your comments with the subject line "Rough Guide Mini Berlin Update" to mail@roughguides.com.

(Abbey in the Oakwood, 1809) and *Der Mönch am Meer* (The Monk by the Sea, 1810). The Friedrich collection is complemented by 15 of Karl Friedrich Schinkel's paintings of imaginative landscapes and architectural visions. Also of interest on the top floor are the lively landscapes, gorges and waterfalls of Carl Blechen, while on other floors, look out for Max Liebermann's *The Flax Workers* and impressionist and post-impressionist works by Monet, Pissarro and Cézanne, alongside Auguste Renoir's striking portrait of comfortable middle class domesticity, *Children's Afternoon at Wargemont*, which are all on the middle floor; and Adolph von Menzel's *Eisenwalzwerk* (The Iron Foundry, 1875), a striking portrayal of industrial labour, on the ground floor.

Further north is the **Pergamonmuseum** ㉑, home to many impressive works of classical antiquity, the Near East, Islam and the Orient. Opened in 1930, the museum has been undergoing extensive renovation since 2013, which is scheduled to stretch well

ARCHITECTS OF BERLIN

An outstanding sculptor and architect, Andreas Schlüter (1664–1714) gave the city much of its Baroque appearance. Look for the 21 masks of dying soldiers in the Zeughaus courtyard (Schlüterhof) in Unter den Linden, and the equestrian statue of Friedrich Wilhelm, 'Der Große Kurfürst' (the Great Elector), outside Schloss Charlottenburg.

Georg Wenzeslaus von Knobelsdorff (1699–1753) was Frederick the Great's favourite architect. Among his greatest achievements are St Hedwigs-Kathedrale, the Staatsoper Unter den Linden, the new wing at Schloss Charlottenburg, and Schloss Sanssouci in Potsdam.

Karl Friedrich Schinkel (1781–1841) was Berlin's most gifted and prolific Neoclassical architect. His other talents were landscape painting and stage design. Works include the Neue Wache and the Altes Museum, the Schauspielhaus at Gendarmenmarkt, and the neo-Gothic war memorial in Viktoria Park, Kreuzberg.

into the 2030s and come with a price tag of up to €1.5bn; the website has details of which parts (if any) are currently accessible. The museum is named after its most prized possession: the gigantic **Pergamon Altar** (second century BC), a Hellenistic masterpiece that came from what is now Bergama, on Turkey's west coast.

The **Babylonian Processional Street** (604–562 BC), built by King Nebuchadnezzar II, is equally impressive. Lions sculpted in relief stride along the street's blue-and-ochre tiled walls towards the Ishtar Gate. The gate itself is decorated with bulls and dragons, also in blue-and-ochre tiles.

A third great treasure is the Roman **Market Gate of Miletus**, from Greek Asia Minor (AD 165). Its name belies the true character of this elaborate monument, which constitutes both a gateway and a shopping complex.

The **Islamic Museum**, part of the Pergamonmuseum, exhibits the grand façade of the eighth-century **Palace of Mshatta** (from what is now Jordan). It is embellished with intricately incised or perforated animal and plant motifs. Among the other exhibits are some exquisite Indian **Mogul miniatures**.

Next to the Pergamonmuseum is the **Neues Museum** 22. Erected between 1843 and 1855 according to plans by Friedrich August Stüler, it was badly bombed in World War II and restored by architect David Chipperfield. It houses the Museum of Prehistory and Early History as well as the **Egyptian Museum**, which covers 3,000 years of sculpture, papyrus fragments and hieroglyphic tablets. The most famous piece in the collection is the beautiful head of **Queen Nefertiti** (1340 BC), consort of Akhenaton. The bust had been buried for over 3,000 years, before German and French archaeologists unearthed it in 1912; it's now reverentially displayed in its own, domed chamber, with restrictions in place on photography. Other highlights of the collection include the Berlin Green Head on the floor below, which depicts an intelligent-looking, middle-aged man with many well-rendered wrinkles and lines on his very realistic, shaved, oval-shaped face; and mummies, sarcophagi, and blue faience funerary objects in the shape of animals.

The final great institution of Museumsinsel, at the very tip of the island, is the **Bodemuseum**, which houses early Christian and Byzantine art, ancient coins, sculpture, and paintings from the Middle Ages to the eighteenth century. The collections here are more rarefied than in the other museums, and the place sees fewer visitors, but look out for, in particular, the collection of fifteenth-century winged altarpieces and the Byzantine apse mosaic from a church in Ravenna, all deep reds and blues against a background of glittering gold.

Berlin Cathedral and around

On the north side of the Lustgarten stands Kaiser Wilhelm II's **Berliner Dom** ㉓ (www.berlinerdom.de/). The imposing exterior has been completely restored, and its interior beautifully renovated, despite heavy bomb damage in World War II. The cathedral's crypt contains 95 Hohenzollern sarcophagi; you can also head up several flights of steps to reach the viewing gallery on the outside of the dome.

Statue on the Schlossbrücke

The Humboldt Forum

On the opposite side of the Lustgarten stands the area once more known as **Schlossplatz**. Under the

The head of Queen Nefertiti

GDR, its name was changed to Marx-Engels-Platz, and it became a focus of communist May Day military parades and rallies. The war-damaged Stadtschloss of the Hohenzollerns once stood here. However, in 1950, Walter Ulbricht decided to raze it as a symbol of German imperialism, despite protests from art historians that it was the city's outstanding Baroque building. The palace balcony where Spartacist leader Karl Liebknecht proclaimed his doomed 'Socialist Republic' in 1918 was added to the front of the former **Staatsrat** (Council of State) on the southeast side of the square, and can be seen to this day, while the bronze, glass and steel Palast der Republik – once East Germany's parliament – replaced what remained of the royal residence (you can see a striking model of it in the DDR museum, close by – see page 73). In 2009, the decaying palace had its date with the wrecking ball, clearing space for the **Humboldt Forum** (www.humboldtforum.org; charge), a venue for exhibitions and theatre shows that is thoroughly contemporary behind the rebuilt Baroque façade of the Stadtschloss, which overlooks the square. The complex includes two museums dedicated to non-European cultures. The **Museum für Asiatische Kunst** (Museum of Asian Art; free) displays treasures from China, Japan, Korea, India, Pakistan, Afghanistan, Sri Lanka, Nepal and Tibet, including delicate paper hangings, wooden screens, paintings, carpets, ceramics and lacquerware, while the **Ethnologisches Museum** (Ethnology Museum; free) focuses on the cultures of ancient America, the South Seas, and South and East Asia, with a special section on Native North Americans and a spectacular presentation on art from Africa.

Immediately beyond the Humboldt Forum the Spree is crossed by the **Friedrichsbrücke** giving access to an expansive urban space that reaches from the DDR Museum and the **Marx-Engels Forum** to the **TV Tower** (see opposite) and beyond, to **Alexanderplatz** (see below).

Alexanderplatz and around

Highlights

- **Marx-Engels Forum and the TV Tower**, see page 72
- **Nikolaiviertel**, see page 73
- **Märkisches Museum**, see page 74
- **Oranienburger Straße**, see page 74
- **Karl-Marx-Allee and East Side Gallery**, see page 75
- **Prenzlauer Berg**, see page 76

'Alex', as Alexanderplatz is known, was the heart of prewar Berlin, and its vibrancy was celebrated in Alfred Döblin's great 1929 novel *Berlin Alexanderplatz*, later filmed by Rainer Werner Fassbinder. In GDR days, the square formed the commercial heart of East Berlin. Renovation work during the Noughties saw the addition of several major buildings, including shopping malls and Berlin's largest underground railway station, and the new building work has continued into the 2020s. Somehow surviving amidst all this is the Weltzeituhr or world clock, which tells the time in various cities around the world, particularly in cities which, in 1969, when it was installed, were in communist countries. It's now a kitschy throwback to GDR days and is the most iconic meeting point in the city.

Marx-Engels Forum and the TV Tower

Heading under the S-Bahn tracks running into and out of Alexanderplatz station you arrive at the iconic **Fernsehturm** ㉕ (TV Tower; https://tv-turm.de/; charge), built in 1969, and at 368m (1,207ft) to this day the highest structure in Western Europe. It was built as a statement in concrete and steel of the permanence of East German control over East Berlin and East Germany as a whole, with the 'golf ball' structure two-thirds of the way up supposedly resembling a Soviet satellite. Not for the fainthearted, an observation deck at 203m (666ft) affords fine views over the city and beyond, while the revolving restaurant provides refreshment.

Beyond the TV Tower is an expansive urban space that stretches to the Spree and the Humboldt Forum. This was once the Neuer Markt, the city's market square. Now it's surrounded by post-1945 developments, with the (clearly) ex-GDR residential blocks along Rathausstrasse a particularly grim eyesore. The focus of the space is the huge **Neptunbrunnen** (Neptune's Fountain) of 1891, an elaborate affair decorated with four figures representing the rivers Rhine, Elbe, Oder and Vistula; it's overlooked from the south by the neo-Renaissance Berliner Rathaus, also known as the **Rotes Rathaus** ㉔ (Red Town Hall), which owes its nickname to its red clinker masonry, not its ideology. Built between 1861 and 1869, it is now the seat of the city's governing mayor and is decorated with a terracotta frieze chronicling the history of Berlin. Head inside and up the grand staircase to an equally grand public room, where there may be exhibitions relating to the city's history. In contrast, overlooking the fountain from the north is the **Marienkirche** (thirteenth century), a haven of sober Gothic simplicity amid the prevailing bombast. Inside, see (behind glass panels immediately inside the entrance) a late-Gothic fresco of the Dance of Death (1484) and, within the church, Andreas Schlüter's Baroque marble pulpit (1703).

The open area between the fountain and the Spree is taken up by the Marx-Engels Forum, a rather severe plaza whose centrepiece is a larger-than-life bronze featuring the two founding fathers of communism; not surprisingly both the statue and the parks are relics from the GDR era – or the end of it, to be precise, because they date from 1986. Speaking of which, to the north, tucked into the east bank of the Spree beside the **Friedrichbrücke**, is the superb **DDR Museum** (www.ddr-museum.de), which provides an intriguing and honest insight into everyday life in the old East Germany, including a mock-up DDR apartment and a Trabant car that can be driven (through some snazzy electronics).

Nikolaiviertel

South of the Rotes Rathaus and Marx-Engels Forum, the Nikolai neighbourhood was restored for Berlin's 750th anniversary celebrations in 1987. The site of Berlin's earliest settlement, the whole district is now a kind of open-air museum. Its focal point is Berlin's oldest church, the twin-steepled Romanesque and Gothic **Nikolaikirche** (www.stadtmuseum.de/museum/museum-nikolaikirche; charge), begun in 1230. Across the road from the entrance is the **Gaststätte zum Nußbaum**, the favourite tavern of cartoonist Heinrich Zille. Some of his works can be seen in the **Heinrich Zille Museum Berlin** nearby (Propststraße 11; https://

Tourists at the Pergamonmuseum

zille-museum.de/; charge). The **Knoblauchhaus**, at Poststraße 23, is an elegant house rebuilt in Neoclassical style in 1835 and containing some fine Biedermeier furniture. Statelier is the reconstructed Ephraimpalais (Poststraße 16), a Rococo mansion built for Friedrich II's financier Veitel Heine Ephraim in 1765. Today, the **Museum Ephraim-Palais** (www.stadtmuseum.de; charge) presents three floors of exhibits on the history of Berlin from earliest archaeological remains through the Middle Ages to the twentieth century.

Märkisches Museum

On the other side of the Spree, across the Jannowitzbrücke, stands the red-brick **Märkisches Museum** (U-Bahn Märkisches Museum; www.stadtmuseum.de/museum/maerkisches-museum; charge). With a wealth of exhibits, the museum tells the story of Berlin from the Middle Ages to the present. The building itself is worthy of attention – its Gothic chapel, guildhall and arms hall have all been restored to their original state.

The Red Town Hall and TV Tower

Oranienburger Straße

On the north side of the River Spree, **Oranienburger Straße** is the heart of the old Jewish quarter. In the 1920s, a diverse community of Jewish professionals and bohemian artists and writers lived, worked and thrived here. The area has regained much of its former vibrancy after the devastation of the war and the grim sterility of its aftermath. Cultural centres and Jewish restaurants rub shoulders with off-beat cafés and alternative art venues beneath the magnificent black-and-gold-leafed dome of the **Neue Synagoge** (https://centrumjudaicum.de/; charge). Once the biggest synagogue in Germany, designed by Eduard Knoblauch and completed in 1866, it was saved during the anti-Semitic attacks of Kristallnacht on 9 November 1938, but was later destroyed by Allied bombing. Its façade has been beautifully restored, and the interior, now rebuilt, is home to a museum about the building's history.

Nearby **Hackesche Höfe** ㉖ is a fascinating complex of early twentieth-century courtyards. Beautifully restored, this is a lively spot, with bars, art galleries, shops, offices, and even a theatre. The adjacent **Anne Frank Zentrum** features an exhibition devoted to the life of Anne Frank (Rosenthaler Straße 39, S-Bahn Hackescher Markt; www.annefrank.de; charge).

Karl-Marx-Allee and East Side Gallery

Known until 1961 as Stalin-Allee, **Karl-Marx-Allee** ㉗ runs southeast from Alexanderplatz. It is worth coming here to look at the façades of the **Stalinesque-style apartment blocks** that line the avenue on both sides, and which, as far as Frankfurter Tor, have been superbly restored. Whether or not you are a fan of the style, you cannot fail to be impressed by the sheer scale of the enterprise.

South of Karl-Marx-Allee along Mühlenstraße, between Ostbahnhof S-Bahn station and Warschauer Straße U-Bahn station, a riverside section of the Berlin Wall has been preserved as the **East Side Gallery** (www.eastsidegallery-berlin.de; free). A variety of international artists painted murals here in 1990, after the collapse of the Berlin Wall, and many of them have since been restored. You can still see some of the iconic images of that era, including *Brotherly Kiss* by Dimitri Vrubel, which depicts a smooching Leonid Brezhnev and Erich Honecker. Next up is the **Wall Museum** (https://thewallmuseum.com; charge), which offers a more off-beat, grittier account of the Berlin Wall's history than the more formal museum near Nordbahnhof station.

Prenzlauer Berg

To the north of Alexanderplatz, Schönhauser Allee leads to the centre of **Prenzlauer Berg**, a nineteenth-century working-class quarter; now a gentrified, bohemian area with colourful nightlife, plenty of cafés and restaurants, and entertainment complexes such as the **Kulturbrauerei** ㉘, a converted brewery. The artist Käthe Kollwitz (see page 78) lived here. A colourful market selling organic produce is held around the central Kollwitzplatz every Thursday and Saturday.

Outside the centre

Highlights

- **Schloss Charlottenburg**, see page 76
- **Olympic Stadium**, see page 80
- **Gedenkstätte Plötzensee**, see page 81
- **Dahlem**, see page 82
- **Grunewald and Wannsee**, see page 83
- **Tempelhof**, see page 86

Schloss Charlottenburg

An exemplary piece of Prussian Baroque and Rococo architecture and decoration, **Schloss Charlottenburg** ㉙ is the city's only surviving major Hohenzollern residence. Badly damaged in a World War II air raid, it became the target of extensive postwar reconstruction and is now the focal point of several of the city's most fascinating museums. To do the palace, grounds and surrounding museums full justice, spend at least a day here. Reach it by U-Bahn

(Richard-Wagner-Platz is 500m away) or by boat tour.

Picturesque street in Nikolaiviertel

Schloss Charlottenburg (www.spsg.de; charge) was conceived as a summer retreat for the future Queen Sophie Charlotte in the 1690s, when the site beside the River Spree, west of the Tiergarten, lay well outside the city limits. It was a small palace – scarcely one-fifth of the huge structure you see today – and only with the addition of a majestic domed tower (with the goddess Fortune as its weathervane), the Orangerie to the west and a new east wing, did it become big enough for Frederick the Great. If he ever had to leave his beloved Potsdam, this was where he came.

In the palace courtyard, you will find an **equestrian statue** of the Great Elector Friedrich Wilhelm, designed by Schlüter in 1697. One of many artworks lost in World War II, it was finally recovered from Tegel Lake in 1949, where it had sunk with the barge that was taking it to safety.

In the **Gobelinzimmer**, notice the fine eighteenth-century tapestries by Charles Vigne. The rays of light on the ceiling of the **Audienzzimmer** (Reception Room) and bright yellow damask walls in the **Schlafzimmer** (Bedroom) imitate the motif of the Sun King, Louis XIV, the Prussian rulers' hero. Chinoiserie is the dominating feature of the opulent **Porzellankabinett**, filled with hundreds of pieces of Chinese and Japanese porcelain. The relatively sober **Japanische Kammer** contains prized lacquered cabinets and tables, and tapestries that depict landscapes in China. The **Eichengalerie** (Oak Gallery) is filled with portraits of the Hohenzollern family. Chamber music recitals can be heard in the **Eosander-Kapelle** (chapel), which has extravagant Rococo decor.

Designed for Frederick the Great by Georg von Knobelsdorff, the **Neuer Flügel** subtly combines dignified late-Baroque façades with exuberant Rococo interiors. The ceremonial staircase that leads to Frederick the Great's state apartments has an abstract modern ceiling fresco by Hann Trier in place of the original decor, which was destroyed by fire. Trier also painted the ceiling of the **Weiße Saal** (throne room and banquet hall).

The finest achievement of Knobelsdorff at Schloss Charlottenburg is the 42m (138ft) long **Goldene Galerie**. This Rococo ballroom, with its marble walls and gilded stucco, leads to two rooms containing a fine group of **Watteau paintings**. Frederick the Great was somewhat amused by the French artist's insolent *Enseigne du Gersaint*, a shop sign for art dealer Gersaint, in which a portrait of Louis XIV is being unceremoniously packed away. Among various other fine works by Watteau, you will find *L'amour paisible* (*Quiet Love*) and *Les Bergers* (*The Shepherds*).

In the western wing of the palace is the intimate **Käthe-Kollwitz-Museum** (www.kaethe-kollwitz.berlin/en/; charge). On display is a comprehensive collection of sketches, drawings and sculptures by the artist Käthe Kollwitz (1867–1945), whose work resounds with compassion as she makes appeals on behalf of the working poor, the suffering and the sick.

When it is time for a break or lunch, make for the **Kleine Orangerie**, then head off to explore the **Schlosspark**. Among the many buildings in the grounds, nearest to the palace is the Italian-style **Neuer Pavillon**, built in 1825 according to plans by Karl Friedrich Schinkel. North of the carp pond, the elegant **Belvedere**, once a teahouse, now contains a collection of exquisite eighteenth- and nineteenth-century porcelain. Also worth visiting in the park is Queen Louise's mausoleum with her marble sarcophagus inside.

Opposite the palace are the two so-called 'Stüler buildings'. The western one is the home of the **Museum Berggruen** (www.smb.museum; charge), an outstanding collection of late nineteenth- and early twentieth-century art assembled by the Berlin-born collector Heinz Berggruen (1914–2007). There are works by many of the great masters of Modernism, but the heart of the collection is formed by dozens of pieces by Picasso. The eastern building is home to the **Sammlung Scharf-Gerstenberg** (www.smb.museum; charge), a collection of Surrealist art. The collection includes paintings, sculptures and drawings by artists such as Goya, Klinger, Redon, Dalí, Magritte, Ernst and Klee. The art is accompanied by a film programme that includes the classic Surrealist films of Salvador Dalí and Luis Buñuel, as well as films by contemporary artists who draw upon Surrealism.

The Neue Synagoge

The private **Bröhan Museum** (www.broehan-museum.de; charge), dedicated to Art Nouveau and Art Deco, is housed in a former infantry barracks opposite the eastern Stüler building. Its peaceful interior makes a fine setting for the array of elegant objects amassed by businessman Karl Bröhan from the 1960s onwards. Highlights include superb ceramics, glassware, silverware and furniture.

Olympic Stadium

Built for the Games of 1936, Hitler's **Olympiastadion** 30 (https://olympiastadion.berlin/de/start/; charge) was spared bombardment, to serve as headquarters for the British Army. The structure's bombastic gigantism is an eloquent testimony to the Führer's architectural taste. Viewed from the main Olympic Gate, it appears surprisingly low slung until you see that the field has been sunk 12m (40ft) below ground level. The 74,000-capacity stadium still

Schloss Charlottenburg

stages sporting events and is open daily to the public at other times. The stadium was modernised in 2006 in preparation for the football World Cup.

West of the stadium, the **Glockenturm** (bell tower; https://glockenturm.de/; charge) gives a magnificent view over the Olympic site. Beyond the tower, a pathway leads to the **Waldbühne** (www.waldbuehne-berlin.de/), an open-air amphitheatre, which is a summer venue for pop and classical concerts.

NOTES

To try to recapture the interior's rather gracious Rococo atmosphere, furniture and decorations from other eighteenth-century Prussian palaces have been used to replace what was destroyed at Charlottenburg during World War II.

On Messedamm, southeast of the stadium, stands another colossus, the famous **ICC** (International Congress Centre). One of the world's biggest convention centres, the complex is also used for staging cultural events. Next to it on the equally huge **Messe und Ausstellungsgelände** (Trade Fair and Exhibition Area), the **Funkturm** (Radio Tower; https://funkturm-messeberlin.de/; charge) is positively tiny; 150m (492ft) to the tip of its antenna, less than half the height of the TV Tower (see page 2). For breathtaking views, take the lift to the restaurant, 55m (180ft) up, or to the observation platform right at the top.

Gedenkstätte Plötzensee

Northeast of Charlottenburg, the **Gedenkstätte Plötzensee** ❸❶ in Hüttigpfad (https://gedenkstaette-ploetzensee.de/; free) is a stark, moving memorial to the victims of Nazi persecution (take bus No. 123 from Turmstraße U-Bahn station or Beusselstrasse S-Bahn station). On the opposite side of the road from the bus stop, a lane leads to the site of the prison where thousands of people were tortured and executed between 1933 and 1945, including many of

(Olympiastadion) Olympic Stadium

the officers involved in the Stauffenberg plot to kill Hitler. Part of the site (clearly visible from the road) is still a prison today.

The dark sheds where executions were carried out have been preserved, and outside a stone urn, filled with soil from concentration camps, stands in a corner of the yard. In one of the sheds, you will find a small and poignant exhibition of historical documents, which includes death warrants and pictures of leading members of the German resistance.

Dahlem

The history of leafy **Dahlem** ㉜ probably goes back for more than 750 years, and something of its rustic character remains, to which the thatched and half-timbered U-Bahn station makes a certain contribution. Opposite the station is one of Berlin's oldest buildings, a manor house dating back to 1560, which is part of the **Domäne Dahlem** (www.domaene-dahlem.de/), a visitor-friendly rural estate with old buildings, a museum, farm animals, well-tended fields, traditional crafts and carriage rides. Dahlem is also an academic and museum district; it was chosen as the site of the Free University set up during the 1948 Airlift as an alternative to Humboldt University in the Soviet sector of the city.

The **Brücke-Museum** (Bus Nos 115 or X10 to Pücklerstraße or Brücke-Museum/Kunsthaus Dahlem from U-Bahn Oskar-Helene-Heim, then 5 minutes on foot from either stop; www.bruecke-museum.de; charge) houses many fine works by early twentieth-century German artists. It was founded in 1967 thanks to the legacy of Karl Schmidt-Rottluff, a member of the Expressionist group *Die Brücke*, which worked in Dresden from 1905 to 1913. A large number of the group's works were labelled as 'degenerate' and thus destroyed by the Nazis. Schmidt-Rottluff's bold paintings hang beside the works of fellow Expressionists Emil Nolde, Erich Heckel, Ernst Ludwig Kirchner and Max Pechstein.

Grunewald and Wannsee

On the western edge of Berlin, the dense pine forest, which was largely stripped for fuel in 1945, has been replanted, adding to the 18 million pines around 6 million chestnut, linden, beech, birch and oak trees. The lush wooded areas form a reserve for deer, wild boar, marten, fox and rabbits, but there are also plenty of green meadows for picnics, and the forest paths are extremely popular with both cyclists and joggers.

The easiest and most direct way to get to the Grunewald is to take the S-Bahn from Bahnhof Zoo to the Grunewald S-Bahn station. Alternatively, you could combine your trip with a visit to the museums at Dahlem; the Brücke Museum is only a 20-minute walk from the eastern edge of the forest. Drivers take the Avus and turn off on the Hüttenweg to **Grunewaldsee** ㉝, a lake offering swimming and

Statue at Charlottenburg Palace

sandy beaches. On the east shore, in an attractive lakeside setting of beech trees, you will find the **Jagdschloss Grunewald** (www.spsg.de; charge), a hunting lodge built in 1542 for Prince Elector Joachim II. Situated in a cobbled courtyard, the lodge has been restored to its original Renaissance appearance. Inside you'll find an exhibition about Berlin portrait painting throughout the centuries, as well as a collection of early German hunting portraits and landscapes, which includes a series of panels depicting the Passion Cycle by Lucas Cranach, as well as works by Jordaens, Rubens and Bruyn.

On the Grunewald's west side, along Havelchaussee, the **Grunewaldturm** (Grunewald Tower; charge) is a striking red brick neo-Gothic lookout tower built in 1897 to commemorate the centenary of the birth of Wilhelm I, with an easy-going restaurant at its foot. Bus No. 218 from Wannsee and Heerstrasse S Bahn stations stops outside. Ferry stations in the area offer boat rides on the River Havel and forest lakes, and the east bank of the Havel is lined with sandy beaches as far as the Wannsee lakes.

The waterfront near **Wannsee** 34 S-Bahn station is a crowded spot where city-dwellers let their hair down on warm spring and summer days. The water bustles with pleasure boats and ferries, and you can cruise to Potsdam from here. **Strandbad Wannsee**, 1.8km (1.1 miles) north of the station (and linked to it by bus

No. 218), is Berlin's biggest beach, and the longest one in inland Europe; a similar distance in the other direction along the shoreline from the station is the vastly more sober **House of the Wannsee Conference** (Haus der Wannsee-Konferenz; www.ghwk.de/eng/; free), a memorial, museum and education centre located in the waterside villa where, in January 1942, fifteen high-ranking representatives of the SS, the Nazi Party and various government ministries gathered to discuss and coordinate the 'Final solution to the Jewish Question' – the deportation and murder of the Jews of Europe. It's not possible to reach the museum by walking along the lake shore; instead, take bus No. 114 from Wannsee S-Bahn, which stops outside.

To the west of the Großer Wannsee, Königstraße crosses Berliner Forst, an extension of the Grunewald to **Glienicke Park**. Its whimsical landscaping of little hills, bridges and ponds was the work of Peter Josef Lenné in the early nineteenth century. **Schloss Glienicke** (www.spsg.de/en/palaces-gardens/object/glienicke-villa; charge) is an Italian-style villa built in 1823 by Prince Carl of Prussia to house his private art collection; today it's still full of art, but visitors can also feast their eyes on the luxurious internal decoration, replete with marble, gold and sparkling chandeliers.

A ferry links **Pfaueninsel** ㉟ (Peacock Island; www.spsg.de/en/palaces-gardens/object/peacock-island; charge), a delightfully tranquil nature reserve in the Havel, to the northern edge of Berliner Forst. The island menagerie was used

NOTES

Berlin's superlative Botanischer Garten (Königin-Luise-Straße 6–8; S-Bahn Botanischer Garten; https://bo.berlin/; charge) is also in Dahlem. Its tropical houses contain some 18,000 species of exotic plants, and there is also a smell and touch garden for visitors with disabilities. A small museum at the north entrance covers the history and use of plants.

to stock Berlin Zoo, but the bird sanctuary still has much to offer the nature-lover, including peacocks, of course.

At the southern tip, half hidden in the trees, is Schinkel's Swiss Cottage, but the island's principal curiosity is the **Schloss Pfaueninsel** folly, built in 1797 as a hideaway for Friedrich Wilhelm II and his lover, the Countess Wilhelmine von Lichtenau. The white wooden façade imitates granite blocks, and the turrets are joined together at the top by a pretty bridge.

Königsstraße extends as far as an illustrious relic of the Cold War, the **Glienicker Bridge**, once a restricted border crossing between West Berlin and East Germany, where the KGB and CIA exchanged spies.

The Dahlem Botanical Gardens

Tempelhof

A working terminal until 2008, **Tempelhof Airport** (U-Bahn Platz der Luftbrücke; www.thf-berlin.de/; guided tours only; charge) to the south of the city centre is an intriguing piece of Berlin's history. Rebuilt in typically stern National Socialist style in the late 1920s, this once vibrant aerodrome was Berlin's main hub during the Nazi era, but was taken over by the US Army in 1945. Probably its finest hour was during the Berlin airlift when the airport buildings were used as the air bridge operations base. The US Air Force

TEUFELSBERG – DEVIL'S MOUNTAIN

At the beginning of the Grunewald, in the middle of the flat, northern European plain that stretches from Warsaw to the Netherlands, is the aptly-named Teufelsberg (Devil's Mountain), which was painstakingly created from a pile of rubble left by World War II bombardments.

In summer, the hill is grassed over for toddler mountain climbers to scramble around on. In winter, snow creates an excellent toboggan run, a good nursery slope for skiers, and even two bone-rattling ski jumps. The flatness of the north European plain east of the mountain is demonstrated by the summit, where radar once scanned as far as Asia. Today the former military facility, and the neighbouring street art gallery, one of the largest in Europe, is open to visitors (www.teufelsberg-berlin.de).

was based here during the Cold War, but when the Berlin Wall came down, the Americans left, and the city chose Schönefeld as its main commercial airport. A must for aviation and history fans alike.

Potsdam

Highlights

- **Sanssouci**, see page 88
- **Schloss Cecilienhof**, see page 90
- **Town centre attractions**, see page 90
- **Einstein Tower**, see page 91
- **Filmpark Babelsberg**, see page 91

Potsdam, 30km (19 miles) southwest of Berlin, and a much older settlement (it was first mentioned as Poztupimi in AD 993), is a real contrast to the capital. A feast for the eyes (and camera lens), it can be heaving with visitors on fine summer weekends – try to visit at a less busy time if possible, and pre-book tickets for the palaces

Sailing on Lake Wannsee, with the Grunewald Tower in the background

too, which operate a timing system. You can get there from central Berlin in a number of ways, but the quickest is by Regional Express train from Bahnhof Zoo to Potsdam Hauptbahnhof. S-Bahn Line 7 also runs to Wannsee, where you can change onto the S1 for Potsdam Hauptbahnhof. To arrive in style, take one of the boat cruises that depart from Wannsee. From Potsdam Hauptbahnhof, visitors heading straight for Sanssouci should take the No. 695 bus, though another way of doing Potsdam is to take the X5 to the Neues Palais and then walk through the extensive park (via Sanssouci and any of the other smaller palaces and pavilions that take your fancy) back to the town centre.

Sanssouci

Potsdam's main attractions are the summer palaces and gardens at Sanssouci, built in the eighteenth and nineteenth centuries. The vast park is filled with charming palaces, pavilions, fountains and temples, but the pièce de résistance is **Schloss Sanssouci** 36 (www.spsg.de for all sites described in this section; charge for each site, or 'Sanssouci+' combined tickets available, either for individuals or families) which was commissioned by Frederick the Great and designed by von Knobelsdorff in 1744 from the king's sketches.

Despite only being single-storey, the 97m (300ft) long garden front is very impressive, with its floor-to-ceiling windows and 35 huge caryatids supporting the roof and dome architrave. Highlights of the magnificent Rococo interior include Frederick's splendid **Konzertsaal** (Concert Chamber), where walls and ceiling are overlaid with delicate gilt filigree; at the centre of the palace, beneath the dome, the **Marmorsaal** (Marble Hall) contains exquisite columns made from Carrara marble and stucco figures on the cornice. Among the guest rooms, the yellow **Voltaire room** is home to some bizarre decorations, including wooden parrots hanging from perches – Frederick's revenge on the famous writer, who was maddened by his master's poor behaviour during his stay at the palace and was openly suspicious of his apparently low intellect.

Nearby, the **Bildergalerie** (Picture Gallery, closed in winter) was designed to house Frederick the Great's collection of paintings by masters such as Caravaggio and Rubens.

A path through the woods southwest of the palace leads to the **Chinesisches Haus** (Chinese House, closed in winter). On top sits a gilded mandarin under a sunshade; inside, you will find a collection of Chinese porcelain.

At the far western end of the Hauptallee, the main route through the park, stands the **Neues Palais** (New Palace), a vast structure built in the 1760s and covered in Rococo statuary. It contains a rich collection of furniture, paintings by Italian, Dutch and French Baroque and Rococo masters, and some fine eighteenth-century ceiling frescoes.

Other highlights of the park include the **Römische Bäder** (Roman Baths), a villa that's a blend of Renaissance Italian country house and Roman architecture unearthed in Pompeii; **Schloss Charlottenhof**, a small palace in classicist style surrounded by a fine landscaped garden; and the vast Italian Renaissance-style **Orangerie**, complete with sculptures, fountains, arcades and terraces outside, and picture galleries and opulent decor inside.

Schloss Cecilienhof

Set beside a lake, 3km (1.9 miles) north of the town centre, English-style park **Neuer Garten** is all very pleasant, but its main draw is **Schloss Cecilienhof** (www.spsg.de/en/palaces-gardens/object/cecilienhof-country-house; charge), the half-timbered pastiche of an English country manor built for Crown Prince Wilhelm and his wife. Winston Churchill, Joseph Stalin and Harry Truman met here in July 1945 to draw up the Potsdam Agreement, which defined how Germany was to be divided for the next 45 years. Unfortunately, the building will be closed for most of the lifetime of this guide for extensive renovation. It can be reached by bus No. 603 from Potsdam Hauptbahnhof.

Town centre attractions

The tram from Potsdam Hauptbahnhof to Alter Markt brings you within a few steps of the Film Museum (www.filmmuseum-potsdam.de; charge), which gives a revealing insight into the workings and history of the town's famous Studio Babelsberg, the cradle of Germany's movie industry. Just 150m away is the neoclassical **Nikolaikirche** (www.nikolai-potsdam.de; free, charge for viewing platform). Designed by Karl-Friedrich Schinkel, its dome bears a striking resemblance to that of St Paul's Cathedral in London and is visible from all over town. The view from the platform that encircles it demonstrates how Potsdam (and similar towns in the former East Germany) have struggled to shrug off the legacy of communist times – identikit residential blocks from that era abound, some even sandwiched between Potsdam's elegant eighteenth-century buildings.

To the north, the old town has three historic gates, the Brandenburger Tor, the Jägertor and the Nauenertor; beyond the latter lies the Baroque Town Hall and the attractive **Holländische Viertel** (Dutch quarter), built for Dutch settlers between 1734 and 1741 by Jan Boumann.

Schloss Sanssouci

Einstein Tower

To the south of the town centre, Albert-Einstein-Straße climbs Telegrafenberg to the amorphous solar observatory **Einsteinturm** (www.aip.de/de/institute/locations/einstein-tower). Designed by the Expressionist architect Erich Mendelsohn (his first major work) and the astronomer Erwin Finlay-Freundlich, its original raison d'être was to prove Albert Einstein's Theory of Relativity. The building is a working observatory, so access is limited, and generally only on tours.

Filmpark Babelsberg

Lights, camera, action. Run as a studio-cum-theme-park, **Filmpark Babelsberg** (www.filmpark-babelsberg.de/; charge), is the perfect place for a peek behind the silver screen with outdoor sets, movie props, stunt shows and 4D cinema.

Berlinale Film Festival

Things to do

In this liveliest of German cities, there is no lack of activities once your sightseeing is done; Berlin has never relinquished its role as the country's capital of the arts or shopping.

Culture

Berliners are assiduous concert- and theatre-goers, so planning ahead is essential if you want good tickets for the main events. Check the listings in city magazine *tipBerlin* (www.tip-berlin.de) and its English-language sister publication *The Berliner* (www.the-berliner.com). Tickets and information on upcoming programmes are also available on the visitBerlin website (www.visitberlin.de).

Classical Music

Classical music in Berlin centres on the Berliner Philharmoniker, one of the world's greatest orchestras. Its principal performance venue is the purpose-built Philharmonie concert hall (see page 51). Other renowned orchestras also perform there, such as the Berliner Staatskapelle and the Deutsches Symphonie-Orchester Berlin. Schinkel's beautifully restored Schauspielhaus on Gendarmenmarkt (known as the Konzerthaus Berlin, see page 61) is another important venue for classical music performances.

Chamber music and *Lieder* (song) recitals take place in the Kammermusiksaal (at the rear of the Philharmonie), and Universität der Künste (Hardenbergstraße 33) hosts masterclasses and chamber music concerts.

Berlin's **opera** lovers are well served by the Deutsche Oper in Bismarckstraße, the Staatsoper Unter den Linden and the Komische Oper, which is performing in several venues across the city while its home in Behrenstraße is undergoing extensive renovation.

Major **rock** concerts are usually performed at large venues such as the Uber Arena (formerly the Mercedes-Benz Arena),

Staatsoper Unter den Linden

Max-Schmeling-Halle, the Velodrom, the open-air Waldbühne and the Olympic Stadium. **Jazz** is particularly popular in Berlin. Venues include Quasimodo (Kantstraße 12a; www.quasimodo.de) and A-Trane Jazzclub (Bleibtreustraße 1; www.a-trane.de). Jazzfest Berlin is an annual jazz festival held in early November.

Theatre and Cinema

Berlin boasts over 140 theatres, and even without a great command of the language, enthusiastic theatregoers can enjoy some memorable and stirring performances.

The city's most controversial theatre performances are staged at the Volksbühne (Rosa-Luxemburg-Platz; www.volksbuehne.berlin), while the Schaubühne (Lehniner Platz on Ku'damm; www.schaubuehne.de) has achieved international renown for its classical, avant-garde and experimental theatre. The plays of Berlin's best-known playwright, Bertolt Brecht, are still performed at the theatre he founded, the Berliner Ensemble (Bertolt-Brecht-Platz 1; www.berliner-ensemble.de). **Contemporary plays** are staged at the Maxim-Gorki-Theater (Am Festungsgraben 2; www.gorki.de), and the **classics** at the Deutsches Theater (Schumannstraße 13a; www.deutschestheater.de). The English Theatre Berlin (Kreuzberg, Fidicinstraße 40; www.etberlin.de) offers a wide variety of quality English-language theatre.

For **popular theatre**, such as musicals, operettas and comedies, try the Theater des Westens (Kantstraße 12; www.berlin-buehnen.de/de/buehnen/stage-theater-westens/) and the Theater at Potsdamer Platz (Marlene-Dietrich-Platz 1; https://tapp.berlin/), as well as the Admiralspalast (Friedrichstraße 101; www.admiralspalast.theater/).

Berlin's largest audience magnet is the **Friedrichstadtpalast** (www.palast.berlin), the only revue theatre in Germany and the largest in Europe. Each production is produced exclusively and performed by the house troupe and orchestra.

As befits a city that every February hosts a major international film festival, Berlin is endowed with a huge number of **cinemas**. Most foreign-language films are dubbed into German, though some cinemas will show films in the original language.

Cabaret

Another long-standing tradition, at its heyday in the 1920s, satirical cabaret has always, by its very nature, had to struggle for existence. Survivors among countless fly-by-nights include Die Stachelschweine (Europa-Center) and Die Distel (Friedrichstraße 101). However, unless your German is excellent, this cabaret will be almost impossible to follow. Bar jeder Vernunft (Schaperstraße 24) and Tipi am Kanzleramt (close to the Chancellery) offer more music-oriented programmes.

Drag shows are another feature of Berlin. Often a mix of drag, variety, comedy and cabaret, they can be saucy, witty and occasionally outrageous.

For something different, lip-synch at **Monster Ronson's Ichiban Karaoke** (Warschauer Straße; www.karaokemonster.de) or enjoy a mix of juggling, aerial acrobatics, comedy and slapstick at **Chamäleon Variete** (Hackesche Höfe; www.chamaeleonberlin.com).

Nightlife

Known for its round-the-clock, open-ended partying, Berlin has hundreds of venues to choose from. Saturday night parties rarely get going before 1am. In summer, beach bars along the River Spree attract the crowds.

Berlin has several nightlife hotspots, one of which is Prenzlauer Berg. A good place to start is **KulturBrauerei** (Schönhauser Allee 36/Sredzkistraße; www.kulturbrauerei.de), a complex of bars, restaurants and theatres on the renovated grounds of an old brewery, offering a vibrant mix of art, music and entertainment. It always draws a crowd.

As the night goes on, choices are limitless. In Mitte, try **Clärchens Ballhaus** (Auguststraße 24; www.ballhausberlinhostel.de), an old-worldly dancehall where Berliners of all ages and walks of life meet to dance the night away. A contrasting venue is the Hotel Adlon Kempinski Berlin's **Lobby Lounge & Bar** (Unter den Linden 77; www.kempinski.com), a sleek bar set beneath a stained-glass dome, soundtracked by a tinkling piano. **Weekend Club Berlin** (Alexanderstraße 7; www.weekendclub.berlin) is a house and techno club on the twelfth and fifteenth floors of a Soviet-style block, with a welcoming atmosphere and a roof terrace. Over on Köpenicker Straße are legendary **Tresor** (www.tresorberlin.com), at No. 70 in an old power plant, and at No. 76 the **Sage Club** (www.sage-club.de), which hosts notorious KitKatClub parties at weekends and has three dance floors, a special pool area and a fire-breathing dragon.

Over in Kreuzberg, **Berghain** (Am Wriezener Bahnhof 1; www.berghain.berlin) is one of the most famous nightclub venues in the world, dubbed 'the world capital of techno' – though potential patrons should thoroughly read up on the place before venturing there for a night out. In the same district, try **Junction Bar** (Gneisenaustraße 18, near U7 stop Gneisenaustraße; www.junction-bar.de), a basement club with live music until DJs take over later in the night. There's a relaxed atmosphere and affordable drinks. A much sleeker venue is **Solar Sky-Bar and Restaurant** (Stresemannstraße 76, through a back alley to the glass lift behind the car park, www.solarberlin.com), a seventeenth-floor bar-lounge near Potsdamer Platz that combines spectacular views (get

Golden hour on the banks of the River Spree

there before sunset) with a fashionable interior and well-mixed drinks. Also in Kreuzberg, **Club der Visionäre** (Am Flutgraben 1, www.clubdervisionaere.com) is the place to chill after a long weekend of partying. Young Berliners relax on boats and floats moored on a canal near Schlesisches Tor underground station.

Shopping

Where to shop

Each of Berlin's many districts has a shopping area, but the city's retail heart remains in the west, on and around the Kurfürstendamm. The Ku'damm itself is lined with trendy boutiques and large department stores such as **Karstadt**. The most famous international designer labels and some exquisite jewellers have luxurious stores on the Ku'damm, particularly between Bleibtreustraße and Olivaer Platz. The cherished institution of **KaDeWe** on Wittenbergplatz, the **Europa-Center** multistorey mall, the good-looking concept mall of **Bikini Berlin** and the redeveloped **Kranzler Eck** with its striking glass skyscraper are close at hand, while elegant shopping streets lead off to the north and south, with a particular focus around Savignyplatz.

In the east, shoppers crowd Friedrichstraße in search of designer labels; the complex of stylish malls known as the Friedrichstraße

GIFT HUNTING IN MUSEUMS

Museum shops are great places to track down art posters, lithographs and high-quality reproductions. In museums of classical antiquity such as the Egyptian Museum and the Pergamonmuseum, you can buy excellent copies of Greek vases or ancient sculpture in bronze, plaster or resin. Museum shops also offer a certain guarantee of quality for genuine artisan products such as textiles, pottery, pewter and woodcarving.

Passagen are always busy. The streets and courtyards north of **Hackescher Markt** have been colonised by a fascinating mixture of fashion boutiques, galleries, antique dealers and bookshops. At the junction of east and west, Potsdamer Platz boasts **Arkaden**, a large indoor shopping centre with more than a hundred shops and supermarkets.

KaDeWe department store

Most of the city's shops are open Monday to Saturday from 9 or 10am until 8pm. However, many outlets, especially in quiet neighbourhoods, may close earlier. Shops are allowed to open from 1 to 8pm on eight Sundays each year, which usually includes those leading up to Christmas.

What to buy

Antiques. Any moderately priced furniture or porcelain that claims to be Baroque or Rococo is probably a copy. Concentrate on items dating from the nineteenth and early twentieth centuries. Some of the side streets off the Ku'damm (such as Fasanenstraße) are the best places to start.

Books. Big general bookshops like Hugendubel (many branches in Berlin, including in KaDeWe and at Kurfürstendamm 231) and Dussmann (Friedrichstraße 90) are lavishly stocked and have some English-language books. Marga Schoeller Bücherstube (Knesebeckstraße 33) has a small, interesting English section.

Mauerpark flea market

Specialist English-language bookshops include Curious Fox (Flughafenstraße 22; www.curiousfoxbooks.com) with new and used English books and Another Country (Riemannstraße 7), which also has a library and hosts events. Shakespeare and Sons (Warschauer Straße 74; www.shakespeareandsons.com) has a wide selection of used English-language titles and the added perk of an in-site café and bagel bakery. The capital is also home to many secondhand and antiquarian bookshops, especially on Schlüterstraße and along Knesebeckstraße.

Bric-a-brac. Berlin has many flea markets (*flohmarkt*; www.visitberlin.de/en/blog/top-11-berlin-flea-markets); each market has its specific days of operation and specialises in certain goods (antiques at the Ostbahnhof market, for example, or books at the Bode Museum). Head to the Turkish Market *(Türkischer Wochenmarkt)* on the Landwehr canal's Maybachufer in Kreuzberg for all manner of wares, as well as to try exotic food, and buy spices and utensils.

Gourmet Delicacies. Among the pastries and cakes that travel best are *Lebkuchen* (gingerbread), *Spekulatius* (spiced Christmas cookies) and marzipan. KaDeWe's *Feinschmeckeretage* (gourmet floor) offers 500 different breads and 1,500 different types of cheese, plus rare eastern delicacies, exotic teas, handmade chocolates and Beluga caviar.

Porcelain. Look for modern Rosenthal and the local Königliche Porzellan Manufaktur (KPM), which was launched by Frederick the Great in the eighteenth century. The KPM shop on the factory premises (Wegelystraße 1 near Straße des 17. Juni) also sells reduced-price seconds. Other celebrated manufacturers represented in Berlin are Meissen (at Unter den Linden 39b), Nymphenburg of Munich and Frankenthal.

Outdoor Activities

Swimming and water sports

The lakes and rivers in and around Berlin provide endless opportunities for **watersports**. It is easy to rent equipment for waterskiing, canoeing, rowing, sailing and windsurfing. Swimmers have around twenty beaches at their disposal, most of them pleasantly sandy. Continuing the old Prussian devotion to physical culture, a few of the beaches are reserved for nude bathing – or FKK, as you may see it signposted. The most popular of these beaches are the Bullenwinkel on the Grunewaldsee, Strandbad Halensee and the Teufelssee. If you would rather wear a swimming costume, try the lovely beaches of the Wannsee, Glienicker See, the Havel, or the less crowded Großer Müggelsee, far in the east of Berlin, and Templiner See, out at Potsdam.

Alternatively, swimmers can head for the Schwimm und Sprunghalle in Europasportpark (Paul-Heyse-Straße 26, Prenzlauer Berg) or the beautiful, ornate Stadtbad Neukölln. The 'Kinderbad Monbijou' in the park opposite the Bode-Museum is a safe pool for small children. Many luxury hotels have pools and spa facilities for recreation.

Participatory Sports

Berlin's sports facilities are second to none, thanks in large part to the huge building programme that took place as part of the city's unsuccessful bid for the 2000 Olympics. There are over 1,500 sports venues in the city, most impressive of which are the Max-Schmeling-Halle and the Velodrom (both in the Prenzlauer Berg district).

Golf enthusiasts can get a round in at the Golf und Landclub Berlin-Wannsee Club (Golfweg 22, www.wannsee.de), as well as at the Golf Club Gatow (www.golfclubgatow.de) in Spandau. You can also hire equipment at both places if you are in need. Golfing for guests is usually restricted to the week, but check online for details.

You can have a go at **indoor climbing** under the supervision of professionals at Magic Mountain in Wedding (Böttgerstraße 20–26; www.magicmountain.de).

In summer, you are likely to encounter a **beach volleyball** game in full swing (such as behind the East Side Gallery in Friedrichshain). Joining in is encouraged.

One surprise sport you may not have expected to practise in Berlin is **hang-gliding,** but it is, in fact, possible to throw yourself off the Teufelsberg, where you can also do a little **skiing** and **sledding** in winter (see page 87).

The most pleasant and effective defence against the aggressiveness of some of the city's **bicycle** goers is to rent a bike yourself and join them.

Spectator sports

The ultimate event in professional football is the final of the football **World Cup**, which Berlin hosted in 2006; the Olympic Stadium underwent a massive refurbishment programme for the big day. The annual **Six Day Cycle Race** has been held every January since 1997 at the Velodrom, while the Uber Arena draws **basketball** fans by the thousands to see the home team, Alba Berlin, take on the opposition. International **tennis** tournaments are held at the Rot-Weiß Club. **'Trotter' horse races** are held at two sites, and last, but by no means least, the **Berlin Marathon** can be enjoyed from the sidelines throughout the city every September.

Children's Berlin

Children are well catered for in Berlin, and many of the things you'll want to do – trips out to the Grunewald, city tours by canal – will also appeal to young ones.

Museums: Some of the city's museums are specifically intended for children, among them the **Labyrinth Kindermuseum** (www.labyrinth-kindermuseum.de/en) and the **MACHmit! Museum** (https://machmitmuseum.de/), both with a whole range of interactive features. Other museums with definite child-appeal include the **Museum für Naturkunde** (see page 47) with its amazing dinosaur skeleton, the **Puppentheater-Museum** (www.puppentheater-museum.de/) offering a behind-the-scenes experience of puppets

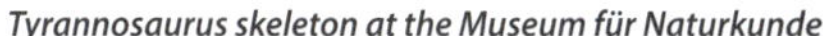

Tyrannosaurus skeleton at the Museum für Naturkunde

Christmas Market on Gendarmenmarkt

and marionettes, and the **Deutsches Technikmuseum** (see page 55) with interactive exhibits on aerospace, engineering and more. At the **Domäne Dahlem** (see page 82) there are craftspeople to watch and animals to admire, while the **Museumsdorf Düppel** (www.stadtmuseum.de/museum/museumsdorf-dueppel) is a re-creation of a medieval village, also with craft and farming activities. There are animals aplenty in Berlin's two zoos, the Zoologischer Garten near the Ku'damm (see page 40) and the Tierpark in Friedrichsfelde (www.tierpark-berlin.de/de).

Parks and play areas: Well-equipped and maintained play areas can be found all over the city, in local neighbourhoods and the many parks. The finest is probably the **Britzer Garten** (www.britzergarten.de/) in Neukölln, with all the usual features plus pools, water playground, animals and a miniature railway. On rainy days, you could try the **Bim & Boom Kinderspielland** (Beilsteiner Straße 109; https://bim-boom.de/), which has climbing towers, tube slides, a ropeway and more.

Other attractions: The actors and spooky sets of the Berlin Dungeon (Spandauer Straße 2; www.thedungeons.com/berlin/) take visitors on a white-knuckle ride through eight centuries of grisly Berlin history, promising great fun for older kids, as will the Planetarium (Prenzlauer Allee 80, Prenzlauer Berg; www.planetarium.

berlin/#/). The Ufa-Fabrik (Viktoriastraße 13–18, Tempelhof; https://ufafabrik.de/) has a children's circus and a farmyard. The Blue Man Group, at the Bluemax Theater on Potsdamer Platz (www.stage-entertainment.de/musicals-shows/blue-man-group-berlin), puts on a colourful show that features a mix of multimedia, percussion, and audience interaction, making it suitable for older kids and their parents. Nearby is the Legoland Discovery Center (see page 105) while on the way to Potsdam, the **Filmpark Babelsberg** (see page 91) will keep the family busy for a whole day.

Festivals and events

For the most up-to-date information on the city's festivals and arts calendar, consult www.visitberlin.de/en/event-calendar-berlin, tourist offices or the listings websites mentioned on page 126.

January: *Berliner Neujahrslauf:* a 4km (2.4-mile) run through the city streets, starting at the Brandenburg Gate (www.berliner-neujahrslauf.de/); SechsTageRennen: a six-day cycle race at the Velodrom (https://sixdayweekend.com/); Internationale Grüne Woche: food and agriculture fair, with specialities from around the world (www.gruenewoche.de/de).

February: *Internationale Filmfestspiele Berlin:* Berlin's International Film Festival rivals those in Cannes and Venice (www.berlinale.de/en/home.html)

March/April: *Festtage:* classical music festival usually held around Easter at the Staatsoper Unter den Linden (in Schillertheater; www.staatsoper-berlin.de/de/).

May: *Theatertreffen:* a German-language theatre festival with productions

NOTES

The Olympic Stadium is the home ground of Berlin's top football club, Hertha Berlin (www.herthabsc.de). Not as well known as clubs like Bayern Munich, it nevertheless enjoys moderate success in the Bundesliga and (occasionally) in European competitions.

from all over Germany, Austria and Switzerland (www.berlinerfestspiele.de/en/theatertreffen). Karneval der Kulturen: three days of multicultural song and dance on the streets of Kreuzberg (www.karneval.berlin/de/).

June: open-air classical music concerts by the Berliner Philharmoniker at the Waldbühne. Christopher Street Day: large LGBTQ+ event with markets, food, performances (https://csd-berlin.de/)

Christopher Street Day

July/August: lots of open-air festivals throughout the city, from the Beer Festival (https://beerweek.de/) to the Köpenicker Blues & Jazz Festival 'Jazz in Town'.

September: *Internationales Stadionfest (ISTAF):* the Olympic Stadium hosts a major track and field event (www.istaf.de/en/).

September/October: *Berlin Marathon* (www.bmw-berlin-marathon.com/); Musikfest Berlin: a major international festival of orchestra and chamber music (Wberlinerfestspiele.de/en/musikfest-berlin).

October/November: *Tag der Deutschen Einheit* (3 October): celebrations to commemorate German reunification; Oktoberfest: beer festival based on the Munich Oktoberfest but smaller and more intimate. Jazzfest Berlin (www.berlinerfestspiele.de/en/jazzfest-berlin).

December: *Weihnachtsmärkte*, including Winterzauber on Potsdamer Platz: Traditional Christmas markets are held on Breitscheidplatz and throughout the city. New Year's Eve party at the Brandenburg Gate.

Food and drink

New German cuisine (*Neue Deutsche Küche*) has emerged in response to a demand for greater culinary refinement. Good old German dishes aren't being replaced by French imitations, but they are being prepared with a new lightness and imagination. Berlin also has a greater variety of cuisines than any other German city, offering everything from Japanese to Hungarian food, along with an extensive range of vegan and vegetarian options.

Top 10 Things to Try

1. Currywurst

Possibly the most famous dish that Berlin has given the rest of the German-speaking world is the currywurst. 'Invented' in 1949 by Herta Heuwer, who began selling it at a food stand in West Berlin, this popular belly filler is simply grilled pork sausage swimming in ketchup and sprinkled with mild curry powder (the curry powder was given to Heuwer by British soldiers). Why this oddly non-Eastern European dish has remained such a beloved snack among Germany's young people in particular is a mystery, though it does hit the spot when hunger strikes after a night out. It's normally sold as street food (from booths or stalls) with chips or bread rolls, using paper plates and disposable wood or plastic forks, though you'll also see it at takeaways and cafes; variations include servings with paprika or chopped onions, and there's also a halal variety, served with beef rather than pork.

2. Sausages

Berlin also claims as its own two world-famous sausages: the giant *bockwurst* (a type of boiled sausage), so named because a local butcher advertised it suspended between the mouths of two goats (*bock*); and the Viennese sausage, or *wiener*, which was invented, so they say, in Berlin. It's served as street food from stalls or in cafés and restaurants.

3. Starters

Appetisers (or starters) can be found listed on the menu under *vorspeisen, kleine gerichte* or *kalte platten.* Classic Berlin starters include *hackepeter,* the German version of steak tartare, and *soleier,* eggs pickled in brine (*sole*), then peeled, halved and seasoned with salt, pepper, paprika, vinegar and oil. They are generally eaten with the ubiquitous Berlin mustard (*mostrich*). You'll also find pretzels on just about every menu, served warm with a big dollop of (you guessed it) Berlin mustard.

4. Soups

You can sample all the traditional German soups (*suppen*) in Berlin. *Leberknödelsuppe* comes with spicy dumplings of flour, breadcrumbs, ox liver, onions, marjoram and garlic. Served at its best, *kartoffelsuppe* is a rich combination of potato, leeks, parsnips, celery and bacon, while *bohnensuppe* is a hearty concoction of several varieties of beans. The city's favourite is plain old lentil soup (*linsensuppe*), best with bits of sausage in it – deliciously hearty and flavoursome.

5. Main dishes: meat

The supreme Berlin meat delicacy is undoubtedly *eisbein mit sauerkraut und erbsenpüree* (pork knuckle on a purée of peas with sauerkraut prepared in white wine, juniper berries, caraway seeds and cloves). Add a generous dollop of mustard, as always. A little humbler, but just as fine, is *gebratene Leber,* also known as *Leber Berliner Art* (sautéed liver served with slices of apple and browned onion rings). The original recipe for *Kasseler rippen* (smoked pork chops) came not from the town of Kassel, but from a Berlin butcher by the name of Kassel.

6. Main dishes: fish

In the best establishments, fish is served fresh from the River Havel. Try specialities like *havelaal grün*, eel boiled in a dill sauce, or *havelzander,* pike-perch served with *salzkartoffeln* (simple but surprisingly tasty boiled potatoes).

Currywurst

7. Asparagus

Asparagus is a vegetable that finds its way onto many Berlin menus. For seven weeks in May and June, Berlin (and most of Germany) goes bananas for *Beelitzer Spargel*, locally-grown white asparagus (Beelitz is a small town to the southwest of Berlin) served with simply with boiled potatoes and melted butter or Hollandaise sauce, accompanied by smoked ham or Schnitzel. The season kicks off with the Primavera Spring Festival on Akazienstrasse in Schöneberg, where you can try the vegetable for yourself in all its glorious variations (there's even a reigning 'asparagus queen' who will answer all your questions about this beloved vegetable).

8. Potatoes

Year-round, potatoes are something of a Berlin obsession. One of the city's great gourmet delights is the *kartoffelpuffer*, a sort of potato pancake often consumed with smoked sausage, sauerkraut and a local beer. *Kartoffelsalat* (potato salad) is also popular.

9. Vegetarian dishes

In this predominantly meat-oriented culture, vegetarians may end up feeling rather excluded. The good news, however, is that most places now include vegetarian dishes on their menus. *Gemüsestrudel* (a type of vegetable strudel) is made from courgettes, onions, sweetcorn, peppers and broccoli in a spicy tomato sauce, and wrapped in flaky pastry. *Ofenkartoffel mit kräuterquark* (baked potato filled with herb-flavoured soft cheese) is also a filling standby. Vegans will find plenty to eat in Berlin's excellent selection of Asian restaurants. There are also many new vegan eateries sweeping through the city, offering veganized versions of German classics and even fine dining.

Kreuzberg eateries

10. Desserts

A very popular dessert is *Rote Grütze* (a delicious compote of raspberries, cherries and blackcurrants), generally served with *vanillesoße* (vanilla sauce). If you want to stretch your waistline, indulge in the German national orgy of Konditorei treats like *schwarzwälder kirschtorte*, the creamy cherry cake from the Black Forest; *apfelstrudel* from Vienna is another favourite dessert. Berliners also love *haselnuss-sahnetorte* (hazelnut cream cake), *käsekuchen* (cheesecake) and *pflaumenkuchen* (Dresden plum cake).

What to drink

Beer

Not surprisingly, Berlin's most popular drink is beer, especially local Berliner Pilsner. Schultheiss and Kindl are the best brews from elsewhere in the country. They are served *vom Fass* (on tap) or bottled in several varieties: *Export,* light and smooth; *Pils,* light and strong; and *Bock,* which is a dark, rich lager. In the summer months, as a refreshing surprise, try the *Berliner Weiße,* a foaming draught beer served up in a huge bowl-like glass complete with a shot (*mit Schuss*) of raspberry syrup or liqueur, or perhaps with *Waldmeister* (green woodruff syrup). Berliners also like the custom of 'chasing' the beer with a shot of Schnapps; any hard, clear alcohol made from potatoes, corn, barley, juniper, or another grain or berry that will distil into something to warm the cockles in the winter months.

Wine and brandy

German wines traditionally come from the south and west of the country. Frederick the Great tried to produce wine at Potsdam but the resulting brew was terrible; still, some winemaking around the city persisted until the World War II and this tradition has undergone a revival since reunification, with the village of Werder, on the Havel just outside Potsdam, being home to vineyards producing highly-regarded Syrah and Cabernet Franc varieties (there's even a tavern at the heart of the vineyards for tasting; https://weinbau-lindicke.de/strausswirtschaft-weintiene/). Some of these wines find their ways onto the menus of Berlin restaurants but it's much more likely you'll encounter wines from elsewhere in the country – the reds cannot be compared in quality to the famous white Rieslings of the Rhine and Mosel valleys but, generally speaking, the whole family of German wines is very respectable.

The most highly regarded German wines are those of the Rheingau. Among the labels to look for are Schloss Johannisberger, Hattenheimer, Kloster Eberbacher, Steinberger and Rüdesheimer. If a celebration is on the cards, you won't go far wrong with a bottle of the champagne-like Sekt. The best of the Rhine Valley red wines come from Assmannshausen and Ingelheim. From Rheinhessen, try the great Niersteiner Domtal and Oppenheimer. Bottled in green glass to distinguish them from the brown Rhine bottles, the Mosel wines enjoy their own delicate reputation. The most celebrated among the varietals include Bernkasteler, Piesporter, Graacher and the Zeltinger.

The brandy (*weinbrand*) made in Germany is not bad, but the very strong fruit Schnapps, which are distilled either from cherries *(kirschwasser)*, plums *(zwetschgenwasser)* or raspberries (*himbeergeist*), are much better and worth sampling. Whatever your poison, 'cheers', or as the locals say, *prost!*

Where to eat

Choices range from high-class restaurants and bourgeois *gaststätten* via the rather chic and arty bistro or café down to the popular *kneipe* (originally student slang for any corner bar or tavern where you can have a drink and a snack big enough to call a meal). All of these places spill out onto the streets and squares as soon as the weather is warm enough; when it is not, there are outdoor heaters.

Berliner Kindl, a popular local beer

The *konditorei* (café/pastry shop) is in a separate category all of its own. In this bourgeois paradise, and armed with a newspaper attached to a rod, you can indulge in the great German tradition of *kaffee und kuchen*. As well as cakes and pastries, ice cream, coffee, tea, hot chocolate, fruit juices and even wines, most places also offer a few light snacks and salads to stave off the hunger pangs. Café Einstein on Unter den Linden is perhaps one of the best places to sit and have breakfast or sample something from a daily selection of mouth-watering cakes. And don't forget the gourmet floor of KaDeWe, where you can sample a dazzling assortment of delicious foods from across the globe (see page 41).

Cafés provide an excellent place to sit and watch the world rush by while you relax. You can order a cup of coffee and then sit for hours without feeling pressured to leave, but it's also possible to fill up in Berlin's cafés for just a few euros.

Brauhaus (literally 'brewery') or *bierkeller,* the old beer-halls, continue to thrive, and become *biergarten* in the parks. Good beer, food and company come as standard.

A menu (*speisekarte*) is displayed outside most restaurants. Besides the à la carte menu, there are generally one or more set menus (*menü* or *gedeck*), which usually work out as pretty good deals. The service charge (*bedienung*) as well as value-added tax

Beelitzer Spargel (white asparagus)

(*mwst*) are usually included; a small tip is sometimes, but not always, expected.

When to eat

Mealtimes are quite flexible in Berlin, and you can always find somewhere to eat at virtually any time of day or night. Breakfast (*frühstück*) generally consists of a selection of rolls, boiled eggs, cheese, muesli and honey, cold meats, fruit juices, *quark* (soft cheese), yoghurt, and either coffee or tea. In hotels, it can be served from as early as 6am until 11am, while many cafés offer a selection of breakfasts from about 9 or 10am until as late as 6pm.

A popular tradition in many eateries is the morning buffet (*frühstücksbuffet*), where you help yourself from the counter to as much as you can eat for a fixed price. Berliners take lunch (*mittagessen*) less seriously than other Germans, probably because the presence of so many fast-food (*imbiss*) places leads to constant snacking. In the evening, restaurants tend to fill up early, and you should reserve in advance for the better establishments.

To help you order

I'd like to reserve a table … **Ich möchte einen Tisch … reservieren**
for two **für zwei Personen**
for this evening **für heute Abend**

A table for …, please. **Bitte einen Tisch für …**
I'd like … **Ich möchte …**
The bill, please **Die Rechnung, bitte**

Menu reader

aal eel
apfel apple
apfelsine orange
aufschnitt cold cuts (charcuterie)
barsch bass
blutwurst blood sausage
braten roast
brot bread
(hühnchen-) brust breast (of chicken)
dorsch cod
ei/eier egg/eggs
eierkuchen pancake
eis ice cream
erdbeeren strawberries
fisch fish
fleisch meat
gans goose
geflügel poultry
gemüse vegetable
heilbutt halibut
himbeere raspberry
hummer lobster
kalb veal
kartoffel potato
käse cheese
kirsche cherry
klosse dumpling
knoblauch garlic
kuchen pie
lachs salmon
lamm lamb
lendenfilet sirloin
milch milk
paprikaschote pepper (vegetable)
pfirsich peach
pflaume plum
pilz mushroom
rinderbraten roast beef
rindfleisch beef
salat salad
salz salt
schinken ham
schweinefleisch pork
seeteufel monkfish
suppe soup
tee tea
thunfisch tuna
truthahn turkey
wasser water
wein wine
weintrauben grapes
wild game/venison
zwiebel onion

Places to eat

As a basic guide, we have used the following symbols to give an idea of the price for a three-course meal for one, including a service charge of 15 percent, but excluding wine.

€€€ = over €55
€€ = €35–55
€ = below €35

West Berlin/Around the Tiergarten

Ashoka Grolmanstrasse 51, www.myashoka.de. During a summer job in 1975, Indian student Ashok Sharma had the idea of transforming an old warehouse into a bistro selling dishes from his native Punjab – and half a century later his imbiss-style eatery attracts everyone from students to business executives who feast on meals such as fresh mixed vegetables in curry cream with almonds and raisins or basmati rice, tamarind chutney, spiced sour milk and salad. **€€**

Bristol Lounge and Eatery Kurfürstendamm 27, www.bristolberlin.com. Luxurious, contemporary bistro inside the Hotel Bristol by Uhlandstrasse U-Bahn, serving European cuisine; alternatively, try the more informal Scirocco, which serves Middle Eastern specialities and has a lovely terrace. There's a dress code for both (see website). **€€€**

Diekmann Meinekestraße 7, www.diekmann-restaurant.de. This Michelin Guide restaurant's interior looks like an old-fashioned store. The German-French-style dishes are cooked with ingredients fresh from Brandenburg's fields, woods and waters – oysters are a speciality. **€€€**

Don Quijote Bleibtreustraße 41 (near Savignyplatz S-Bahn stop), http://donquijote-berlin.de. This lively, long-established Spanish restaurant is notable for its excellent food and friendly atmosphere. **€€**

Gasthaus Krombach Meinekestraße 4, www.gasthaus-krombach.de. A homely, wood-panelled pub-restaurant with a vaguely 1920s feel and a tempting menu of schnitzel, sauerkraut and other German comfort food. Wash it down with one of the seven beers on tap, including Berlin pilsner. **€€**

Marjellchen Mommsenstraße 9 (two blocks from Savignyplatz), www.restaurant-marjellchen-berlin.de. An intimate, welcoming establishment specialising in unusual dishes from East Prussia (historically part of the German Empire but now divided between Russia, Lithuania and Poland); expect plenty of warming soups (such as beetroot or potato) plus lots of meaty mains, though there are also some good vegetarian options and salads. **€€**

Ottenthal Restaurant & Weinhandlung Kantstraße 153, www.ottenthal.com. Hearty Austrian cuisine done right, with superb schnitzels, steaks, and veal carpaccio, as well as an assortment of delicious vegetarian dishes. The apple strudel might be the best in Berlin. **€€**

Paris-Bar Kantstraße 152 (near Zoologischer Garten station), https://parisbar.net/. Classic French and international cuisine in an intellectual/arty atmosphere. A Berlin institution. **€€**

Qui Potsdamer Straße 3, www.themandala.de/en/bar/food/. This stylish bistro in the Mandala Hotel is heavy on meat dishes, though salads and vegan options are available. **€€**

Route 66 Pariser Strasse 44, https://route66diner.de/. A traditional 1950s American diner (though probably larger than many along Route 66), complete with jukeboxes, flashing neon, shiny red benches and photos of Elvis (only the soccer matches on the big tellies suggest you may not actually be in Missouri). The menu includes enormous burgers and sandwiches, along with pasta and salads, and there's even pancakes with maple syrup for breakfast. **€€**

La Sepia Marburger Straße 2 (not far from Europa-Center), www.lasepia-berlin.de. This cosy Spanish-Portuguese restaurant specialises in tapas and fish dishes, mainly grilled. Has a great, friendly atmosphere. Very reasonable lunch specials. **€€**

Wintergarten im Literaturhaus Fasanenstraße 23, https://cafe-im-literaturhaus.de/. This haven of peace is situated in the Literaturhaus villa and is the perfect place to collect your thoughts. The idyllic salon at the back is ideal on sunny days; in summer, the garden doubles as an extra room. **€€**

Kreuzberg

Chutnify Pflügerstraße 25 (nearest U-Bahn is Hermannplatz), www.chutnify.com. Chutnify offers a lighter and creative take on South Indian traditional street food, including the popular *masala dosa*. There is also a branch at Stredzkistraße 43. **€€**

Curry 36 Mehringdamm 36, http://curry36.de. Quintessentially postwar West Berlin, the currywurst (grilled sausage, doused in ketchup and sprinkled with curry powder) is as popular as ever and the best place to try a waxed tray of the stuff is this café near the Mehringdamm U-Bahn station – the place is so venerable that it's 'practically a world heritage site' (according to them). **€**

Henne Leuschnerdamm 25 (four blocks from U8 Moritzplatz stop), www.henne-berlin.de. Not that keen on chicken? Then you haven't tried the *milchmasthähnchen* (milk-fed chicken) here, almost the only fare on the menu. People flock to this unpretentious old Berlin wirtshaus for it. Make a reservation. **€**

Hostaria del Monte Croce Mittenwalder Straße 6 (near U7 Gneisenaustraße stop), www.hostaria.de. This tiny restaurant offers copious portions of genuine northern Italian food in an authentic atmosphere. Make a reservation. **€€**

Osteria No.1 Kreuzbergstraße 71 (near Victoriapark), www.osteria-uno.eu/en. A lively ambience combined with good trattoria fare keeps the regular young crowd flocking back for more. There's an inviting garden with a playground, too. Reservations are highly recommended. **€€**

Central Berlin/Around Unter den Linden

Berliner Republik und Brokers Bierbörse Schiffbauerdamm 8 (at Friedrichstraße station, western exit), www.die-berliner-republik.de. Big and breezy beer hall on the banks of the River Spree. As well as a good choice of solidly good and unpretentious food, there is an amazing range of beers, the prices of which go up and down on a screen as the demand fluctuates. **€**

Borchardt Französische Straße 47 (off Gendarmenmarkt), www.borchardt-restaurant.de. An elegant, airy restaurant with a 1920s atmosphere, conveniently situated just off the historic Gendarmenmarkt. Generous portions and a daily changing menu. In fine weather, diners eat outside at tables set out on the pavement. **€€€**

Brauhaus Georgbrau Spreufer 4, www.georgbraeu.de/. The beer garden of this riverside microbrewery is the place to come for specialist home-brews and homestyle German cooking. Enjoy Berlin-style rissole or bratwurst with a light pilsner or dark lager, in classic local style. **€€**

Brechts Steakhaus Schiffbauerdamm 6–7 (near Friedrichstraße station, western exit), www.brechts.de. Grill specialities made with high-quality Irish beef alongside freshly prepared salads, vegetarian dishes (including a burger made from pea protein), fish dishes (such as salmon steak) and unique desserts. **€€**

Café Einstein Unter den Linden 42, www.einstein-udl.com/. The original 'Einstein Café' in Berlin – there are now several spread through the city – is popular with the city's cultural elite and not surprisingly, given its location, with tourists; this stylish, old-school place is great for everything from breakfast to lunchtime Austro-Hungarian dishes to coffee and cakes in the afternoon. **€€**

Gaffel House Berlin Dorotheenstraße 65, www.gaffel-haus-berlin.de. Boisterous Rhenish (Rhineland) beer bar (the place is nicknamed the 'Cologne Consulate') with hearty stews, salmon fillet, apple strudels and ice-cold kölsch beer on the menu. **€€**

Käfer Dachgarten Restaurant im Reichstag Platz der Republik 1, www.feinkost-kaefer.de/pages/dachgarten-restaurant-berlin. Reserving a table in this restaurant is a great way to bypass the long queues for the Reichstag cupola. The fine meals come with a spectacular view. Bring your passport to get into the building. **€€€**

Lorenz Adlon Esszimmer Unter den Linden 77, at Hotel Adlon Kempinski, www.kempinski.com/en/hotel-adlon/restaurants-bars/lorenz-adlon-esszimmer. Berlin dining doesn't come more refined than this elegant restaurant in the Hotel Adlon Kempinski, overlooking the Brandenburg Gate. Chef Jonas Zörner has won awards for his exquisite brand of modern gourmet cuisine combined with Asian flavours – the menu includes dishes such as wild turbot with fennel, pepper and tomato or organic duck liver with truffle, hazelnuts and bananas. Reservations essential. **€€€**

Lutter & Wegner Charlottenstraße 56, https://l-w-berlin.de/. This elegant Berlin institution, which has been on the go since 1811, serves up meat and fish dishes such as veal liver in port wine and onion sauce with braised apple, roasted onions and potato purée (there are also vegetarian options) – with apple strudel for afters. Tables spill out onto the pavement for fine-weather dining. **€€**

Ständige Vertretung Schiffbauerdamm 8, www.staev.de/berlin-mitte.html. Next door to the Berliner Republik, this cheerful establishment has an intriguing political theme, with photos, posters and much else decorating the walls. Serving typical Rhineland dishes and delicious hoppy kölsch beer from Cologne, it's a welcoming home from home for politicians and civil servants exiled from the former seat of government in Bonn. **€**

Unsicht-Bar Berlin Saarbrücker Straße 36-38, www.unsicht-bar-berlin.de. The food here is served in complete darkness by blind waiting staff. The idea is that removing sight gives your other senses, including taste, the chance to take over. Dishes include dal curry, vegan cream soup of roasted cauliflower and celeriac, and Salmon tartare with braised carrots and seaweed. **€€€**

Weihenstephaner Neue Promenade 5, www.weihenstephaner-berlin.de. Part of the Weihenstephaner brewery, this eatery on the square next to Hackescher Markt S-Bahn has dirndl-clad waitresses and serves hearty and satisfying Bavarian specialities at affordable prices. In fine weather, the outside tables allow for plenty of people-watching on the busy square. **€€**

Zille-Stube Spreeufer 3, www.zillestube-nikolaiviertel.de/en. This traditional German restaurant honours the artist Heinrich Zille, whose illustrations adorn the wood-clad walls. A suitably authentic atmosphere complements dishes such as knuckle of pork with potatoes and sauerkraut or calf's liver with apple slices and onion rings – or you can opt for a classic Berlin currywurst with fries. **€€**

Zur Letzten Instanz Waisenstraße 14–16 (near U2 stop Klosterstraße), www.zurletzteninstanz.com. Berlin's oldest restaurant, founded in 1621, serves delicious regional cuisine and offers great set menus or buffets for travel groups. **€€**

Further afield

Azzam Sonnenallee 54 (near U7/8 stop Hermannplatz). This Neukölln institution doesn't look like anything special from the outside, but it is one of the best places in Berlin to enjoy Lebanese cuisine. The fresh homemade hummus is worth the trip alone, but the shawarma and falafel deserve a mention too. **€**

Blockhaus Nikolskoe Nikolskoer Weg 15, Wannsee, http://blockhaus-nikolskoe.de. Classic German cuisine (with Rhineland dishes a speciality) in an old dacha originally built for Tsar Nicholas I. The setting is lovely, with views over the Havel and Peacock Island. **€€**

CODA Dessert Dining Friedelstraße 47 (near U7/8 stop Hermannplatz), www.coda-berlin.com. From its origins as a dessert bar in 2016, this sleek establishment has evolved into a self-described 'non-conformist fine dining restaurant with two Michelin stars'. Chef René Frank applies patisserie techniques to create unique dishes using exotic ingredients like chicory and medjool dates. Reservations essential. **€€€**

Eiffel Ku'damm 105 (western end of the avenue), https://eiffel-restaurant.de. As the name implies, this is a French restaurant, though definitely with a Mediterranean touch. The wood and steel interior is as sleek as the dishes on offer. **€€**

Nauta Kastanienallee 49 (near U2 stop Senefelderplatz), http://nautaberlin.com. This fashionable restaurant specialises in Nikkei cuisine – a blend of Japanese and Peruvian. It sounds unlikely, but dishes like grilled octopus with corn, chorizo and black garlic are delicious. The eye-catching décor brings to mind an 1980s arcade game. **€€€**

Pasternak Knaackstraße 22–24 (near U2 stop Senefelderplatz), www.restaurant-pasternak.de. In the trendy neighbourhood of Prenzlauer

Berg, this restaurant (named after Boris Pasternak, the author of *Doctor Zhivago*) plates up typical Russian fare to a mixed crowd of artists and intellectuals revelling in its authentic atmosphere. **€**

Roji – Taste of Japan Mühlenstr. 1 (U-Bahn and S-Bahn Pankow), www.pankow.roji-berlin.de. Great sushi in the trendy neighbourhood of Pankow, in a wood-panelled restaurant where dishes include the likes of crayfish tartare with baby asparagus topped with flambéed salmon, salmon tartare and sesame, or 'prawn attack' featuring five king prawns, salmon, avocado, cucumber, cream cheese, tobiko and sesame. **€€**

Rutz-Zollhaus Carl-Herz-Ufer 30, Kreuzberg, www.rutz-zollhaus.de. New German Cuisine, served in an idyllic green setting on the bank of the old Landwehrkanal. The timber-framed rustic building even has a boat landing, while the innovative cooking includes dishes such as braised ox shoulder with pea puree and roasted wild broccoli, mushrooms, onions and pea cress. **€€**

Udagawa Feuerbachstraße 24, Steglitz (near S1 station Feuerbachstraße), https://restaurant-udagawa.jimdofree.com/. Excellent Japanese cuisine, especially the seafood options, which include grilled seabream in teriyaki sauce. Reservations essential. **€€**

Travel essentials

Practical information

Accessible travel

Berlin is one of the most accessible cities in Europe, with well-adapted public transit and user-friendly public buildings and spaces. Berlin's official travel portal, visitBerlin, has a dedicated accessibility section (www.visitberlin.de/en/accessible-berlin) with comprehensive information on accommodation, restaurants, sights and transport. There is also a wealth of information available on Mobidat (www.mobidat.net; in German only), the city's searchable database of access guides.

Accommodation

If you are coming to Berlin for a trade fair or convention or want to enjoy the old-world, elegant charm of a bourgeois neighbourhood, the Charlottenburg area (in former West Berlin) is probably for you. If it's all about seeing the sights, Mitte (in former East Berlin) is the go-to district. It's much closer to the famous Museum Island, Potsdamer Platz and the historic city centre. The less central areas of Mitte and Prenzlauer Berg offer more affordable accommodation, plenty of nightlife and more opportunities to mix with the locals. If you prefer a peaceful location, consider Spandau or the Grunewald. Alternatively, you can stay in one of Potsdam's charming hotels, close to the palaces and gardens, and only about an hour from Berlin.

I'd like a single/double room **Ich möchte bitte ein Einzel-/Doppelzimmer**
... with a bathroom/shower **... mit Bad/Dusche**
How much per night/week? **Wie viel kostet es pro Nacht/Woche?**

Airport

Berlin Brandenburg Airport Willy Brandt (Flughafen Berlin Brandenburg Willy Brandt; www.berlin-airport.de) lies about 19km (12 miles) southeast of the city centre and serves as the city's sole airport, with flights operated by carriers from low-cost airlines such as easyJet, Wizz Air, Ryanair and Eurowings through European airlines such as Lufthansa, British Airways and Aer Lingus to long-haul carriers flying to the United States or the Persian Gulf.

The airport's train station is located beneath Terminal 1. It is connected to the Hauptbahnhof by Airport Express trains and regional trains (RE8); regional trains also run direct to Alexanderplatz (RE8 and RB23), Spandau (RE8), Wannsee (RB23) and Potsdam (RB22; also served by Bus BER2, which links the airport to Potsdam central station). S-Bahn S9 trains run from the airport to Spandau, Charlottenburg, the Hauptbahnhof, Alexanderplatz and Treptower Park – the other S-Bahn line serving the airport, S45, is less useful for visitors. The U-Bahn network does not extend to the airport, however, Express Buses X7 and X71 will transport you to Rudow U-Bahn station on line 7. Some intercity services also run direct from the airport's railway station to Dresden, Rostock and many other cities in northeast Germany. A taxi to the city centre (a 35-minute drive) costs approximately €55.

Where can I get a taxi? **Wo finde ich ein Taxi?**
How much is it to the centre/Potsdamer Platz? **Wie viel kostet es ins Zentrum/zum Potsdamer Platz?**
Is this the bus to the Ku'damm? **Ist das der Bus nach zum Ku'damm?**

Apps

visitBerlin curates a list of visitor apps (www.visitberlin.de/en/berlin-websites-and-berlin-apps), including 'Going Local Berlin' (an insider's guide to Berlin's neighbourhoods with over 700 listings) and 'About Berlin' (the story of the city from 1871 to the present day).

Bicycle rental

Bicycle lanes are usually marked by red or grey bricks between the pavement and the road, often with a bike drawn on them. Rental companies include Berlin Bike Rental (Knaackstraße 97; https://berlinonbike.de/en/bike-rental), app-based nextbike (https://www.nextbike.de/berlin/en), Fahrradstation (Mehringdamm 29; www.fahrradstation.com) and Fat Tire (Panoramastraße 1a; www.fattiretours.com/berlin/berlin-bike-rentals).

Budgeting for your trip

The following list will give you some idea of the approximate prices to expect in Berlin. The sales tax for most goods and services (normally included) is 19 percent.

Public Transport: See page 137 under 'Transport' for more details of ticket prices

Entertainment. Cinema: €9–13, theatre: €13–45, club: €6–20.

Hotels (double room per night). Luxury class €275–500, first class €170–275, medium range €90–165, budget class €45–90.

Hostels. Beds in dorms from €15, typically €20–30, double rooms with shared bathroom from €40 (per person).

Meals and drinks. Breakfast €6–22, lunch or dinner in fairly good establishment €22–50 (check out the lunch offers), bottle of wine (German) €22–33, beer (half-litre) €4–5, soft drink (small bottle) €3–4, coffee €3–4.

Museums. Around €7–14, with reductions for students and free entrance to state museums for under 16s. The three-day Berlin Museum Pass (€32) offers admission to the museums on Museumsinsel, together with around thirty other museums in the city (purchase at participating museums, tourist offices or online at www.smb.museum/en/plan-your-visit/museum-pass). Valid for two to six days, the Berlin WelcomeCard (see page 138) provides reductions of up to 50 percent on entry prices for many major attractions (buy online at www.berlin-welcomecard.de/en or purchase at tourist offices).

Car hire

The best way to hire a car is online before you leave home to get the best possible rates. If you wait to hire a car upon arrival at Berlin Brandenburg Airport Willy Brandt, with one of the major international companies, you'll pay for the pleasure. Average turn-up-and-drive costs: VW Polo €65 per day, BMW3 €95 per day.

You'll need a valid driving licence (held for at least one year) and a credit card. The minimum age is typically 21, but some companies may set a higher minimum age.

All car hire companies listed have branches at the airport and the Hauptbahnhof.

Avis, Budapester Straße 43; www.avis.de.
Europcar, Alexanderplatz 8; www.europcar.de.
Hertz, Friedrichstraße 50–55; www.hertz.de.
Sixt, Budapester Straße 45; www.sixt.de.

I'd like to rent a car **Ich möchte bitte ein Auto mieten**
... tomorrow **... für morgen**
... for one day/week **... für einen Tag/für eine Woche**
Please include full insurance **Bitte schließen Sie eine Vollkaskoversicherung ab**

Climate

Berlin's climate follows the continental pattern of cold, snowy winters and agreeably warm summers with low humidity. The best time to visit is late spring or summer when temperatures tend to be mild.

Average temperatures are as follows:

	J	F	M	A	M	J	J	A	S	O	N	D
°C												
max	2	3	8	13	19	22	25	23	20	13	7	3
min	-3	-3	0	4	8	12	14	13	10	6	2	-1
°F												
max	35	37	46	56	66	72	75	74	68	56	45	38
min	26	26	31	39	47	53	57	56	50	42	36	29

Crime and safety

Berlin is generally a very safe city, with a crime rate of 13,500 per 100,000 people. Take the same precautions as you would at home. Report an incident at the nearest police station. The police will give you a certificate to present to your insurance company or consulate if your passport has been stolen.

Driving

To enter Germany with your car, you will need the following: a national driving licence, car registration papers, a national identity sticker for your vehicle (except for cars with EU licence plates), a red warning triangle in case of breakdown, reflective safety jackets, beam deflectors and a first-aid kit.

Insurance. Third-party insurance is compulsory. Visitors from abroad, except those from the EU and certain other European countries (including the UK), will have to present their international certificate (Green Card) or take out third-party insurance at the border.

Driving conditions. Rush-hour traffic jams and a dearth of parking spaces make driving in central Berlin somewhat frustrating. At the beginning and end of peak holiday periods, bottlenecks tend to form on approach roads into Berlin, but traffic generally flows. Drive on the right, pass on the left. Seat belts are obligatory.

Speed limits. The speed limit in Germany is 100km/h (60mph) on all open roads except motorways and divided highways, where there's no limit unless indicated – the suggested maximum speed is 130km/h or 80mph. In town, speed is restricted to 50km/h (30mph) or 30km/h (20mph). Cars with trailers may not exceed 80km/h (50mph).

Traffic police. Police may confiscate the car keys of persons they consider unfit to drive. The permissible blood-alcohol level is 0.5mg per ml.

Breakdowns. For round-the-clock breakdown service, call ADAC Auto Assistance, tel: 22 22 22 (from a mobile); tel: 01802 22 22 22 (from a landline); or tel: 112 (general emergency number).

Fuel and oil *(Benzin; Öl)*. You'll find petrol stations everywhere, the vast majority of them self-service. Many are open 24 hours.

Umweltzone. Vehicles entering the environmental zone (inside the Berlin S-Bahn ring) must carry a low-emission sticker, which can be obtained from the vehicle registration office or authorised garages.

Einbahnstraße one-way street
Fußgänger pedestrians
Kurzparkzone short-term parking
Rechts fahren keep right
Parken verboten no parking
Umleitung detour
Vorsicht caution
Führerschein driving licence
Kraftfahrzeugpapiere car registration papers
Grüne Versicherungskarte green (insurance) card

Electricity

Germany has 220–250 volt, 50-cycle AC. Plugs are the standard continental type, so British and North American devices need an adaptor. American devices may require a voltage converter.

I need an adaptor/battery, please **Ich brauche bitte einen Adapter/eine Batterie**

Embassies and consulates

Australia: Wallstraße 76–79, 10179 Berlin; tel: 030-88 00 880.
Canada: Leipziger Platz 17, 10117 Berlin; tel: 030-20 31 20.
Ireland: Jägerstraße 51, 10117 Berlin; tel: 030-22 07 20.
South Africa: Tiergartenstraße 18, 10785 Berlin; tel: 30-22 07 30.
UK: Wilhelmstraße 70–71, 10117 Berlin; tel: 030-20 45 70.
US: Pariser Platz 2, 10117 Berlin; tel: 030-830 50.

Emergencies

The following emergency services are available 24 hours:

Police: **110**

Fire: **112**

Ambulance: **112**

Non-emergency medical assistance: **116 117**

Air rescue: **(0711) 70 10 70**

I need a doctor **Ich brauche einen Doktor**
an ambulance **einen Krankenwagen**
a hospital **ein Krankenhaus**

Getting there

By air. There are direct daily flights to Berlin Brandenburg Airport Willy Brandt from major airports all over Europe (and further afield from China and the Middle East); however, travel from North America (except New York and Toronto) often requires a change of aircraft in Frankfurt or another European city. From the UK and the Republic of Ireland, the cheapest fares are usually available through budget airlines Ryanair and easyJet, which offer very low fares if booked early. In terms of routes, British Airways flies into Berlin from Heathrow and London City; Aer Lingus from Dublin; Ryanair and easyJet from Luton, Stansted, Gatwick, Dublin and several regional UK cities; Delta and United from New York (JFK and Newark); and Air Transat from Toronto.

By rail. Eurostar services from London St Pancras take you to Brussels, where you can travel to Berlin with one change – usually in Cologne but possibly in Frankfurt or elsewhere. Overnight services link Berlin with France and Northwest Germany; routes change regularly, though have in the past included sleeper trains operating between Paris and Berlin (14 hours).

By bus. Coaches run by FlixBus from London Victoria take about 23 hours to reach Berlin – probably with a change of vehicle on the way, though there are some direct services.

By road. Berlin is 579 miles (931km) from Calais, 446 miles (718km) from Hook of Holland, 430 miles (692km) from Rotterdam and 424 miles (682km) from Ijmuiden near Amsterdam.

By ferry. There are no direct ferries from the UK to Germany, but travellers can route through Holland (Harwich to Hook of Holland or Newcastle to Amsterdam).

Guides and tours

If required, the tourist office will put you in touch with qualified guides and interpreters for personally conducted tours.

City sightseeing tours by bus are an excellent introduction to Berlin, and most companies offer multilingual recorded commentary. Daily excursions by coach to Potsdam and the Spreewald are also available, as are weekend trips to other places in Germany, including Dresden and Wittenberg. Hop-on, hop-off sightseeing tours depart from the Kurfürstendamm, between Rankestraße and Fasanenstraße:

City Circle (https://city-circle.de/en). Candy-coloured, open-top hop-on, hop-off tour bus with 26 stops including the Brandenburg Gate, Museum Island, Reichstag, Alexanderplatz and the Kurfürstendamm.

City Sightseeing Berlin (www.berlin-city-tour.de). Choose from the 18-stop 'Classic' tour or the 12-stop 'Trendy East Berlin and the Wall' tour, which picks up from the Ostbahnhof and Alexanderplatz.

videoSightseeing (www.videosightseeing.de). Film, photos and sound material make this time-travel shuttle an inspiring adventure in history. There's a wide choice of shorter or longer trips, departing from a number of locations including the Nikolaiviertel and Charlottenburger Ufer (near Schloss Charlottenburg).

Reederei Bruno Winkler (www.reedereiwinkler.de/en). This company offers a variety of routes by boat through the day and evening, some with meals served on board.

Stern und Kreis Schiffahrt (www.sternundkreis.de). Routes for boat cruises include those that thread through the city's suburbs (from

Treptown Park) as well as the centre; there are also party-based cruises with live music.

There are also several very good English-language walking tour operators in the city, including **Sandemans New Europe** (www.neweuropetours.eu/berlin-walking-tours), which offers free tours; **Original Berlin Walks** (www.berlinwalks.com); and **Insider Tour** (www.insidertour.com). All offer private or public tours including a general city tour, alongside tours with specific themes such as Jewish Berlin, the Third Reich, street art, Queer Berlin and Communist Berlin; they also offer tours using public transport that visit Potsdam and the Sachsenhausen Concentration Camp, north of the city.

For a self-guided tour of Berlin focusing on where the Wall was, choose from one of many apps available through the visitBerlin website (see page 139).

Health and medical care

It's important to ake out travel insurance before you arrive in Berlin. UK citizens may use the German Health Services for medical treatment on presentation of a UK Global Health Insurance Card (available online through the NHS). The equivalent for EU citizens is the European Health Insurance Card (available through national health insurance providers of relevant countries).

In the event of an accident or serious illness, call for an ambulance (tel: 112) or ask the medical emergency service (tel: 116 117) to recommend a good local doctor.

Pharmacies are open during normal shopping hours. They are marked with a red 'A' for Apotheke. At night, on Sundays and holidays, all pharmacies display the address of the nearest open one.

Where's the nearest (all-night) pharmacy? **Wo ist die nächste Apotheke (mit Nachtdienst)?**
What would you recommend for ...? **Was empfehlen Sie bei ...?**

Language

Although you can expect many of the people you meet in the west of the city to speak English, this will not necessarily be the case in the east, apart from the 'trendy' areas.

Greet people with *guten Tag* and say goodbye with *auf Wiedersehen* or *tschüß* (the latter is less formal). The word for 'please' is *bitte* (also used in the sense of 'you're welcome'). 'Thank you' is *Danke schön*.

LGBTQ+ travellers

Berlin has a thriving LGBTQ+ scene, with the high point being the Christopher Street Day Parade in June. Most venues are around Nollendorfplatz in Schöneberg. visitBerlin has details for LGBTQ+-friendly hotels (see page 126).

Lost property

Berlin's lost-property office (*Zentrales Fundbüro*; tel: 030 902 77 31 01) is at Platz der Luftbrücke 6 in the building of the former Tempelhof Airport. If you left something on public transport, contact the BVG (tel: 030 29743333) at Rudolfstraße 1-8, near the Warschauer Straße station.

Money

Currency. Euro (EUR/€) notes are denominated in 5, 10, 20, 50, 100 and 500 euros; coins in 1 and 2 euros and 1, 2, 5, 10, 20 and 50 cents.

Changing money. The easiest way to obtain euros is at an ATM. Foreign currency can be changed at ordinary banks (*Bank*), savings banks (*Sparkasse*) and currency exchange offices (*Wechselstube*). Hotels, travel agencies and the central post office also have exchange facilities, but rates are much less favourable.

I want to change some pounds/dollars **Ich möchte Pfund/Dollar wechseln**

Where's the nearest bank/currency exchange office? **Wo ist die nächste Bank/Wechselstube?**

Is there a cash machine near here? Gibt **es hier einen Geldautomaten?**
How much is that? **Wieviel kostet das?**

Opening times

Most shops are open Monday to Saturday between 10am and 8pm. A few supermarkets in or around railway stations are open on Sunday.

Banking hours are usually Monday to Friday from 9am to 3pm. Most banks remain open one or more afternoons a week; however, days vary. The currency exchange office of the ReiseBank in the Hauptbahnhof is open daily from 9am to 7pm.

Most museums in Berlin are closed on Monday; the exception is official museums and memorial centres that commemorate the Nazi or Communist era which tend to be open daily. Some attractions outside the city centre (such as some of the Potsdam palaces) might only be open from Easter to October.

Police

Germany's police officers wear dark blue uniforms. You'll see them on white motorcycles or in blue-and-silver cars or vans. The police emergency number is **110**.

Where's the nearest police station? **Wo ist die nächste Polizeistation?**
I've lost my ... **Ich habe ...**
wallet/bag/passport **meine brieftasche/meine tasche/ meinen reisepass verloren**

Public holidays

The chart below shows the public holidays celebrated in Berlin when shops, banks, official departments and many restaurants are closed. On 24

December (Christmas Eve), shops stay open until noon, but most restaurants, theatres, cinemas and concert halls are closed.
1 January **Neujahr** (New Year's Day)
1 May **Tag der Arbeit** (Labour Day)
3 October **Tag der Deutschen Einheit** (Reunification Day)
25–26 December **Weihnachten** (Christmas)
Moveable dates:
Karfreitag (Good Friday)
Ostermontag (Easter Monday)
Christi Himmelfahrt (Ascension Day)
Pfingstmontag (Whit Monday)

Telephones

The dialling code for Germany is 49. The dialling code for Berlin from outside the city is 030. Drop the first zero when calling from outside the country.

Enquiries: tel:11 8 33 (domestic); tel: 11 8 34 (international).

Time zones

Germany follows Central European Time (GMT +1) from the last Sunday in October until the last Sunday in March, when the country switches to Central European Summer Time (GMT +2).

New York	London	**Berlin**	Jo'burg	Sydney	Auckland
6am	11am	**noon**	noon	8pm	10pm

Tipping

Since a service charge is normally included in hotel and restaurant bills, tipping is not obligatory, although it is gladly accepted.

Toilets

Herren indicates 'Gentlemen' and *Damen* indicates 'Ladies'.

Where are the toilets? **Wo sind die Toiletten?**

Tourist information

visitBerlin (www.visitberlin.de) operates several **information points** in the city.

Brandenburger Tor, South Wing; daily 10am–6pm.

Hauptbahnhof (Central Station), Floor 0/Entrance North, Europa Platz 1; daily 8am–9pm.

Airport, Level EO, Terminal 1; daily 9am–9pm.

Humboldt Forum, Entrance via Schlossplatz; daily 10am–6pm.

See www.visitberlin.de/en/tourist-informations-districts for details of information offices in Treptow, Pankow, Spandau and Neukölln.

In addition to free maps, lists and brochures, Berlin's tourist offices sell the Berlin WelcomeCard (see page 138) and museum tickets; tickets for the theatre and other events can also be purchased.

The German National Tourist Board website (www.germany.travel/en/home.html) also provides much useful information.

Transport

Berlin is served by an efficient network of buses, trams, U-Bahn (underground railway), S-Bahn (suburban railway), and Regionalbahn (regional railway), administered by the *Berliner Verkehrsbetriebe* (BVG). The U-Bahn currently covers the inner city and many outlying districts, while the bus service reaches nearly every corner of Berlin. The S-Bahn (operated by Deutsche Bahn) provides an efficient link to places further afield such as the Grunewald, Wannsee, Potsdam and Köpenick, and its central, overhead section linking Savignyplatz, Zoologischer Garten, Friedrichstraße and Alexanderplatz is particularly useful. The tram network operates mainly in the former East Berlin.

The **U-Bahn** operates from 4am to 1am Sunday to Thursday; Friday and Saturday, most lines run all night. U-Bahn stations are marked by a white 'U' on a blue background, and S-Bahn stations by a white 'S' on a green background.

Buses and **trams** run at least 20 hours a day at 10-minute intervals (every 20–30 minutes at night). Night bus routes coincide with the U-Bahn network. Bus stops are easily recognisable by a yellow sign marked with a green 'H'.

When's the next bus to...? **Wann geht der nächste Bus nach...?**
Will you tell me when to get off? **Könnten Sie mir bitte sagen, wann ich aussteigen muss.**

Tickets are interchangeable between trains, buses and trams, entitling you to free transfers for up to two hours (no return allowed). Ticket machines are yellow (U-Bahn) or red (S-Bahn) and sell the same tickets; there's an English language option on the machines, and all take cash and cards. There are also ticket offices at some stations. Tickets can also be purchased via the BVG ticket app (www.bvg.de/en/subscriptions-and-tickets/all-apps/ticket-app). Tickets are date-stamped the moment you buy them, so don't purchase them in advance. Paper tickets need to be stamped at the start of your journey in one of the red or yellow machines *(entwerter)* on station platforms and buses. You can also buy a ticket on the bus itself (card only). The most cost-effective option is to buy either a one-day ticket (*tageskarte*, €10.60 for zones A and B, €11.20 for zones B and C or €12.30 for zones A, B and C) or a one-day group ticket (*kleingruppenkarte*, €33.30, €34.40 or €35.50, depending on the zones). They both allow travel up to 3am the day after the ticket is stamped at an *entwerter*, and the group ticket covers up to five people. A ticket for zones A and B will suffice for most journeys. Travelling to Potsdam or the airport requires a zone C ticket. Holders of a Berlin WelcomeCard (see page 127) are also entitled to free public transport during the validity of the card, so long as they buy the version of the card that includes public transport.

Deutsche Bahn (German Rail) trains are comfortable and fast. EC (EuroCity) are international trains; IC (InterCity) and ICE (InterCity Express) are long-distance national trains. First-class travel on the Deutsche Bahn costs double the second-class fare. A supplement is charged for travel on EC, IC and ICE trains. Children under 6 travel free in Germany, while 6- to 14-year-olds go free if travelling with fare-paying adults; otherwise, they pay half fare. The German Rail Pass (https://int.bahn.de/en/offers/german-rail-pass) allows unlimited travel in Germany for any three to fifteen days within one month.

Long-distance buses depart from the Zentraler Omnibusbahnhof Berlin (ZOB; https://zob.berlin/en) near the Funkturm (Radio Tower) in Messedamm.

In Berlin, **taxis** are mostly cream-coloured Mercedes – book through your hotel or contact Taxi Berlin (www.taxi-berlin.de) – but **rickshaws** (www.biketaxi.de) are also part of the city landscape, especially around busy tourist areas like Potsdamer Platz and Brandenburg Gate.

Where can I get a taxi? **Wo finde ich ein Taxi?**

Visas and entry requirements

Citizens of Schengen Area member states can enter Germany without a visa, but must be able to identify themselves with a valid passport or national identity card. At the time of writing, nationals of third countries with visa-waiver agreements can enter Germany for short stays (up to 90 days within any 180 days) provided they have a valid passport (issued within the last ten years and in date for at least three months after the departure date), however, they will have to apply for a travel authorisation through the ETIAS system before their trip from 2026 on. Nationals from third countries without a visa-free agreement will need to apply for a Schengen visa before entry.

Index

U1 Uhlandstrasse–Warschauer Strasse
U2 Pankow–Ruhleben
U3 Krumme Lanke–Nollendorfplatz
U4 Nollendorfplatz–Innsbrucker Platz
U5 Hauptbahnhof–Hönow
U6 Alt-Tegel–Alt-Mariendorf
U7 Rathaus Spandau–Rudow
U8 Wittenau–Hermannstrasse
U9 Rathaus Steglitz–Osloer Strasse
Airport bus
S1 Wannsee–Oranienburg
S2 Blankenfelde–Bernau
S25 Teltow Stadt–Hennigsdorf
S26 Teltow Stadt–Waidmannslust
S3 Erkner–Spandau
S41 S42 Ringbahn
Oranienburg
Lehnitz
Borgsdorf
Birkenwerder
S8
Hohen Neuendorf
S85
Bergfelde
Frohnau
Waidmannslust
Hermsdorf
Wittenau
Hennigsdorf
Heiligensee
Schulzendorf
Tegel
Alt-Tegel
Borsigwerke
Holzhauser Str.
Otisstr.
Scharnweberstr.
Kurt-Schumacher-Platz
Afrikanische Str.
Rehberge
Seestr.
Amrumer Str.
Karl-Bonhoeffer-Nervenklinik
Rathaus Reinickendorf
Wilhelmsruh
Eichborndamm
Alt-Reinickendorf
Schönholz
Lindauer Allee
Paracelsus-Bad
Residenzstr.
Franz-Neumann-Platz (Am Schäfersee)
Osloer Str.
Wollankstr.
Nauener Platz
Leopoldplatz
Pankstr.
Altstadt Spandau
Zitadelle
Haselhorst
Paulsternstr.
Rohrdamm
Siemensdamm
Halemweg
Jakob-Kaiser-Platz
Beusselstr.
Westhafen
Gesundbrunnen
Jungfernheide
Wedding
Reinickendorfer Str.
Humboldthain
Birkenstr.
Schwartzkopffstr.
Nordbahnhof
Oranienburger Str.
Naturkundemuseum
Spandau
Rathaus Spandau
Mierendorffplatz
Ruhleben
Olympia-Stadion
Neu-Westend
Westend
S46
Stresow
Turmstr.
Oranienburger Tor
Hauptbahnhof
Pichelsberg
Theodor-Heuss-Platz
Kaiserdamm
Sophie-Charlotte-Platz
Richard-Wagner-Platz
Deutsche Oper
Tiergarten
Bellevue
Bundestag
Friedrichstr.
Unter den Linden
Olympiastadion
Heerstr.
Messe Nord/ICC
Messe Süd
Westkreuz
Wilmersdorfer Str.
Bismarckstr.
Ernst-Reuter-Pl.
Brandenburger Tor
Potsdamer Platz
Savignyplatz
Hansaplatz
Mendelssohn-Bartholdy-Park
Mohrenstr.
Zoologischer Garten
Anhalter Bahnhof
Charlottenburg
Uhlandstr.
Kurfürstenstr.
Gleisdreieck
S5
Halensee
Adenauerplatz
Kurfürstendamm
Wittenbergplatz
Nollendorfplatz
Bülowstr.
Möckernbrücke
Grunewald
Augsburger Str.
Viktoria-Luise-Platz
Spichernstr.
Hohenzollernplatz
Konstanzer Str.
Güntzelstr.
Bayerischer Platz
Kleistpark
Yorckstr.
Fehrbelliner Platz
Hohenzollerndamm
Eisenacher Str.
Berliner Str.
Rathaus Schöneberg
Julius-Leber-Brücke
Blissestr.
Heidelberger Platz
Rüdesheimer Platz
Bundesplatz
Innsbrucker Platz
Schöneberg
Südkreuz
S45
Breitenbachplatz
Podbielskiallee
Friedrich-Wilhelm-Platz
Dahlem-Dorf
Walther-Schreiber-Platz
Friedenau
Freie Universität
Priesterweg
Oskar-Helene-Heim
Schlossstr.
Feuerbachstr.
Südende
Attilastr.
Onkel Toms Hütte
Krumme Lanke
Lankwitz
Rathaus Steglitz
Mexikoplatz
Schlachtensee
Botanischer Garten
Marienfelde
Buckower Chaussee
Nikolassee
Wannsee
Zehlendorf
Sundgauer Str.
Lichterfelde West
Lichterfelde Ost
Schichauweg
Osdorfer Str.
Lichtenrade
Griebnitzsee
Babelsberg
Teltow Stadt
Lichterfelde Süd
Mahlow
Potsdam Hauptbahnhof
S7
Blankenfelde